**Better Homes and Gardens** ®

# MONEY-SAVING MEALS

© Copyright 1986 by Meredith Corporation, Des Moines, Iowa.
All Rights Reserved. Printed in the United States of America.
First Edition. First Printing.
Library of Congress Catalog Card Number: 85-73120
ISBN: 0-696-02193-5

## BETTER HOMES AND GARDENS® BOOKS

**Editor** Gerald M. Knox
**Art Director** Ernest Shelton
**Managing Editor** David A. Kirchner
**Copy and Production Editors** James D. Blume, Marsha Jahns, Rosanne Weber Mattson, Mary Helen Schiltz

**Food and Nutrition Editor** Nancy Byal
**Department Head, Cook Books** Sharyl Heiken
**Associate Department Heads** Sandra Granseth, Rosemary C. Hutchinson, Elizabeth Woolever
**Senior Food Editors** Julia Malloy, Marcia Stanley, Joyce Trollope
**Associate Food Editors** Barbara Atkins, Linda Henry, Mary Jo Plutt, Maureen Powers, Martha Schiel, Linda Foley Woodrum
**Recipe Development Editor** Marion Viall
**Test Kitchen Director** Sharon Stilwell
**Test Kitchen Photo Studio Director** Janet Pittman
**Test Kitchen Home Economists** Jean Brekke, Kay Cargill, Marilyn Cornelius, Jennifer Darling, Maryellyn Krantz, Lynelle Munn, Dianna Nolin, Marge Steenson, Cynthia Volcko

**Associate Art Directors** Linda Ford Vermie, Neoma Alt West, Randall Yontz
**Assistant Art Directors** Lynda Haupert, Harijs Priekulis, Tom Wegner
**Senior Graphic Designers** Jack Murphy, Stan Sams, Darla Whipple-Frain
**Graphic Designers** Mike Burns, Sally Cooper, Brian Wignall, Kimberly Zarley

**Vice President, Editorial Director** Doris Eby
**Executive Director, Editorial Services** Duane L. Gregg

**President, Book Group** Fred Stines
**Director of Publishing** Robert B. Nelson
**Vice President, Retail Marketing** Jamie Martin
**Vice President, Direct Marketing** Arthur Heydendael

### Money-Saving Meals
**Editor** Maureen Powers
**Copy and Production Editor** Marsha Jahns
**Graphic Designer** Tom Wegner
**Electronic Text Processor** Donna Russell
**Photographer** Michael Jensen and Sean Fitzgerald
**Food Stylists** Suzanne Finley, Dianna Nolin, Janet Pittman, Maria Rolandelli

**On the cover**
Mini Loaves with Beer-Cheese Sauce (see page 26)

Our seal assures you that every recipe in *Money-Saving Meals* has been tested in the Better Homes and Gardens® Test Kitchen. This means that each recipe is practical and reliable, and meets our high standards of taste appeal.

Looking for a way to keep your budget afloat and still keep your crew from jumping ship? Start here! We'll show you how to create all kinds of delectable dinners, scrumptious suppers, and luscious lunches in *Money-Saving Meals,* a cookbook designed for the cost-conscious you.

Each chapter, featuring a complete menu, presents a different cost-cutting idea. A timetable takes you through the menus step by step, so you're assured of serving hot dishes, piping hot; and chilled dishes, icy-cold. In addition, be sure to sneak a peak at the tips, hints, and techniques we've included to help you trim the budget. By whittling away lots of little costs, you'll wind up saving a bundle and at the same time enjoy the delicious, wholesome dishes you demand.

# Contents

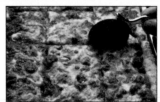

### Meat Plus Rice
**24**

Two old favorites, ground beef and rice, team up to stretch meat further and save you cents!

### Souper Supper
**30**

Creative and money-saving to boot! Use one or up to six types of dried beans in this hearty, satisfying meal in a bowl.

### Make-Ahead Brunch
**36**

Stretch food dollars by turning leftovers into a snazzy meal.

### Affordable Beef Dinner
**42**

Slow-cooking an economical cut of meat makes it fork-tender—just like its expensive counterparts.

### Harvesttime Dinner
**72**

Bountiful fruits and vegetables highlight this autumn feast.

### Dinner from The Freezer
**78**

Individual meals at your fingertips—from freezer to table in less than 45 minutes!

### Ham On Sale
**84**

Chowder, kabobs, and baked ham slices are three delectable ways to take advantage of this supermarket special.

### Versatile Chicken
**90**

Wow! Two chickens give you three delicious ways to enjoy a money-saving meal.

### Money-Saving Moxie
**118**

**Special Helps**
Super suggestions to help you cut food costs.

### Picking Produce
**120**

**Special Helps**
Terrific tips to make you a pro at fruit and vegetable selection.

### Nutrition Analysis Chart
**122**

### Index
**125**

# Brown Bag Lunch

Toting a lunch saves you money, but it sure makes for dull meals. Right? Wrong.

No more "ho-hum" lunches for you. Instead, create our creamy chicken-and-cheese-stuffed pita rounds for your midday mainstay. Then, pack some fresh fruit, a container of milk, and homemade cookies for an unbeatable noontime break.

## Menu

- Chicken and Cheese Pockets*
- Fresh fruit
- Oat Wafers*
- Milk

*see pages 8-11

*Chicken and Cheese Pockets*

# Chicken and Cheese Pockets

*Middle Eastern pita bread (also called pocket bread) has a wonderfully chewy texture and its pocket makes a nifty holder for sandwich fillings.*

| | |
|---|---|
| 1 | **3-ounce package cream cheese** |
| ½ | **cup shredded cheddar cheese (2 ounces)** |
| 1 | **cup diced cooked chicken *or* turkey** |
| 1 | **8-ounce can crushed pineapple, drained** |
| 1 | **tablespoon snipped parsley** |
| 1 | **teaspoon prepared mustard** |
| ¼ | **teaspoon celery seed** |
| 2 | **large pita bread rounds, halved crosswise** |
| | **Lettuce leaves** |

In a mixing bowl soften cream cheese (see photo 1). Stir together cream cheese and cheddar cheese, then stir in chicken or turkey, pineapple, parsley, mustard, and celery seed (see photo 2).

Divide the filling among 4 freezer containers. Seal, label, and freeze for up to 1 month.

For each brown bag lunch, place 1 pita half in a clear plastic bag (see photo 3). Wrap a lettuce leaf in another clear plastic bag. Place 1 container of filling, a pita half, and lettuce in a brown bag with other lunch items and a frozen ice pack. At serving time, place lettuce in pita, then add filling (see photo 4). Makes 4 sandwiches.

**1** In a medium mixing bowl soften the cream cheese with a wooden spoon. Use the back of the spoon to press the cheese against the side of the bowl until the cheese is soft enough to mix.

**2** Using the same bowl and spoon, stir the cheddar cheese into the cream cheese. Then stir in the chicken or turkey, drained pineapple, parsley, and seasonings until they're thoroughly combined.

**3** Pack a pita half and a lettuce leaf in separate plastic bags or plastic wrap. Seal both tightly to make sure the lettuce stays crisp and the pita half stays soft.

**4** Pack the container of frozen filling along with an ice pack in the morning. By noontime, the filling should be thawed, but still very cold.

Remember to take along a small plastic spoon, too. When you're ready to eat, add the lettuce to the pita half, then spoon in the filling.

# Timetable

**1** day before

- Make Oat Wafers, as shown; cool. For individual brown bag servings, place several wafers together in clear plastic bags. (Make the cookies whenever you have some time. Cool, wrap, then store in the freezer. They'll keep for up to a year.)
- Stir together the sandwich filling; divide it among four freezer containers. Freeze.

**6** hrs. before

- Pack the pita and lettuce separately. Fill an insulated vacuum bottle with cold water, as shown. Replace the lid and let stand for 5 minutes. Empty the bottle; fill it with cold milk.
- Pack a brown bag with milk, frozen ice pack, container of filling, plastic spoon, pita half, lettuce, fruit, and Oat Wafers. Keep in a cool place till lunchtime.

## At Serving Time

- Line the pita bread half with lettuce, then spoon in the chicken and cheese filling. The filling should be thawed, but still icy cold.

# Oat Wafers

*Cut the dough into pie-shape wedges with a fluted pastry wheel for wafers with an attractive, crinkly edge.*

1⅓ cups rolled oats
1 cup all-purpose flour
⅓ cup toasted wheat germ *or* bran
¼ cup sugar
¼ cup packed brown sugar
¼ teaspoon ground cinnamon
⅓ cup margarine *or* butter
½ cup orange juice
2 tablespoons sugar
1 teaspoon ground cinnamon

Place oats in a blender container or food processor bowl. Cover, then blend or process for 1 minute or till oats are evenly ground. In a large mixing bowl combine oats, flour, wheat germ or bran, ¼ cup sugar, brown sugar, and ¼ teaspoon cinnamon. Cut in margarine or butter till the mixture resembles coarse crumbs. Stir in orange juice till moistened. Cover and chill the dough about 2 hours.

Divide dough into 8 portions. On a floured surface, roll 1 portion into a 6-inch circle; keep remaining dough in the refrigerator. With a pastry wheel or knife cut the dough into 8 pie-shape wedges. Place wedges on lightly greased baking sheets. Repeat with remaining dough.

Stir together 2 tablespoons sugar and 1 teaspoon cinnamon. Sprinkle atop wedges. Bake in a 375° oven for 8 to 10 minutes or till wedges are light brown around edges. Makes 64.

# Cherry-Chip Turnovers

*For another brown bag dessert, substitute a cherry-chocolate turnover for the wafer cookies.*

2½ cups all-purpose flour
½ teaspoon salt
⅔ cup shortening
6 to 8 tablespoons cold water
1 21-ounce can cherry pie filling
¼ cup semisweet chocolate pieces
Milk
Sugar
Ground cinnamon

In a medium mixing bowl stir together flour and salt. Cut in shortening till pieces are the size of small peas. Sprinkle *1 tablespoon* water over part of mixture; gently toss with a fork. Push to side of bowl. Repeat till entire mixture is moistened. Form dough into a ball.

Divide dough into 12 balls. On a lightly floured surface roll each ball into a 5-inch circle. For filling, in a small mixing bowl stir together pie filling and chocolate pieces. Spoon about *3 tablespoons* of filling onto half of each pastry circle. Moisten edges of pastry with a little water and fold other half of dough over filling. Seal edges with the tines of a fork.

Place turnovers on ungreased baking sheets. Prick tops of turnovers 2 or 3 times with a fork. Brush with a little milk; sprinkle with sugar and cinnamon. Bake in a 375° oven about 35 minutes or till golden. Cool. Wrap individually in moisture- and vaporproof wrap. Seal, label, and freeze for up to 3 months.

For a brown bag lunch, place a wrapped frozen turnover in bag with other lunch items and a frozen ice pack. Turnover should be thawed by lunchtime. (*Or,* to serve warm for a meal at home, arrange frozen turnovers on an ungreased baking sheet. Bake in a 400° oven about 10 minutes or till warm.) Makes 12.

# Easy-Does-It Supper

Looking for a meal that has it *all?* Call off the search! Our supper is easy to make, inexpensive, and most important, it's fantastic tasting.

We used budget-wise convenience foods to create a light, refreshing meal. What's the star? A main-dish salad!

## Menu

- Speedy Tuna Salad*
- Melba toast
- Pickle spears
- Upside-Down Sugar-and-Spice Cake*
- Milk

*see pages 14–17*

*Speedy Tuna Salad*

# Speedy Tuna Salad

| | |
|---|---|
| 1 | 8-ounce carton plain yogurt |
| ¼ | cup snipped parsley |
| 1 | teaspoon sugar |
| ¼ | teaspoon onion powder |
| ¼ | teaspoon dried dillweed |
| 1 | medium head lettuce |
| 2 | ounces American cheese |
| 2 | cups frozen cut green beans, cooked, drained, and chilled |
| 1 | large tomato, cored and chopped |
| 1 | 12½-ounce can tuna, chilled and drained |

For dressing, in a small bowl stir together yogurt, parsley, sugar, onion powder, and dillweed (see photo 1). Cover and chill while preparing the salad. Core lettuce (see photo 2). Rinse lettuce, then drain well. Tear lettuce into bite-size pieces. Cube cheese (see photo 3).

In a large salad bowl combine lettuce, cheese, and green beans. Spoon dressing over salad and toss. Add tomato. Flake tuna into the salad bowl (see photo 4). Gently toss salad. Serves 6.

**1** Stir the dressing ingredients together in a bowl to evenly distribute the seasonings throughout the dressing before they're added to the salad. Cover; chill while preparing the rest of the salad.

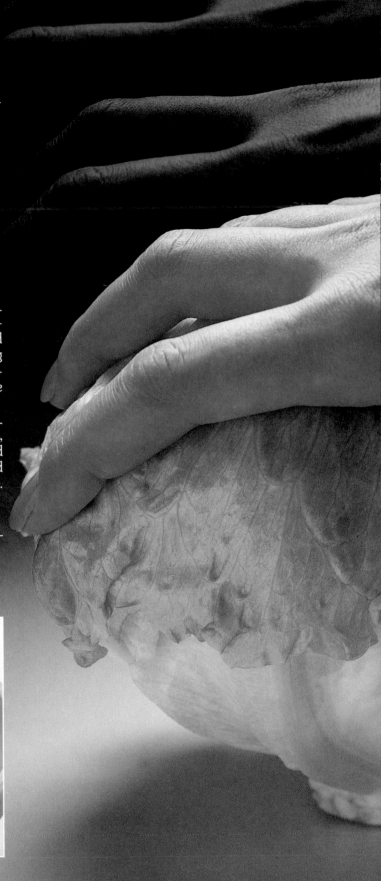

**2** Loosen the lettuce core by hitting the stem end on a counter. Twist the core, then pull it out and discard it. Rinse and drain.

**3** To quickly slice the cheese into cubes, first cut the cheese into fingerlike sticks. Stack the cheese sticks, then cut across them to form evenly sized cubes.

**4** To drain the tuna in the can, press the loosened lid against the fish, then invert the can. Using a dinner fork, flake the tuna right from the can into the salad, breaking the tuna into bite-size pieces.

# Timetable

**1** hr. before
- Prepare the dressing for the salad. Chill it in the refrigerator until you're ready to add it to the salad.
- Start the cake by arranging the apple slices in a circular pattern in the butter-sugar mixture, as shown. Sprinkle with nuts, then carefully pour the cake batter over the apple slices. Bake.

**30** min. before
- Set the table. Arrange melba toast in a small basket. Fill a small serving dish with pickles.
- Core, rinse, and drain the lettuce for Speedy Tuna Salad. Tear the lettuce into a salad bowl. Add the cheese and green beans. Spoon the dressing over the entire mixture, as shown, then toss. Add the chopped tomato and flaked tuna.

**Just Before Serving**
- Remove the cake from the oven. Loosen the edges all the way around the pan with a knife. Place a serving plate on top of the baking pan, as shown, then invert the cake onto the plate. Carefully remove the pan.
- Pour the milk. At the table, gently toss the salad with the dressing to coat all of the ingredients.

# Upside-Down Sugar-and-Spice Cake

*An amazingly simple way to turn a cake mix into a special dessert!*

¼ cup margarine *or* butter
¼ cup packed brown sugar
1 medium apple, cored and cut
  into thin slices
¼ cup finely chopped pecans
1 package 1-layer-size spice cake mix

Place margarine or butter in an 8x1½-inch round baking dish or pan. Place the baking dish in a 350° oven for 3 to 4 minutes or till margarine or butter is melted. Remove from the oven. Stir in sugar till dissolved. Arrange apple slices in a circle in the bottom of the prepared dish. Sprinkle with pecans.

Prepare cake mix according to package directions. Carefully pour cake batter over apples and nuts in the baking dish or pan. Bake in a 350° oven for 25 to 30 minutes or till cake tests done when a wooden toothpick inserted in the center comes out clean. Cool for 5 minutes on a wire rack.

To remove cake, loosen sides from the dish. Invert cake onto a serving plate. Serve warm. Makes 6 servings.

# Tutti-Frutti Cobbler

*A quick-fixin' cobbler, featuring refrigerated biscuits and canned fruit—a perfect dessert substitute for the cake.*

1 package (6) refrigerated biscuits
2 tablespoons sugar
⅛ teaspoon ground cinnamon
1 tablespoon cornstarch
¼ teaspoon ground cinnamon
½ cup orange juice
1 17-ounce can chunky mixed fruit *or*
  one 16-ounce can fruit cocktail

Use kitchen shears to cut the biscuits into quarters. In a plastic or paper bag combine sugar and ⅛ teaspoon cinnamon. Add biscuit quarters; shake to coat. Set aside.

In a small saucepan combine cornstarch and ¼ teaspoon cinnamon; stir in orange juice. Add *undrained* chunky mixed fruit or fruit cocktail. Cook and stir till the mixture is thickened and bubbly.

Immediately transfer the hot fruit mixture to a 1-quart casserole; top with biscuit pieces. Bake in a 400° oven about 15 minutes. Serve warm. Makes 6 servings.

# Dinner In a Dish

One-dish meals are great. Minimal preparation and quick cleanup make them so easy.

To keep the budget in line, make your one-dish combo with ground meat. Need new ways to use that old standby? Try our wonderful suggestions— they're more than just the ordinary fare.

## Menu

- Meat and Spinach Range-Top Casserole*

- Garden Marinade*

- Rolls and butter

- Ice cream with Strawberry Sauce*

- Hot tea

*see pages 20-23

*Meat and Spinach Range-Top Casserole*

# Meat and Spinach Range-Top Casserole

1 **10-ounce package frozen chopped spinach**
3 **slices rye bread**
3 **tablespoons margarine *or* butter**
1 **pound ground pork *or* ground beef**
½ **cup chopped onion**
1 **cup milk**
2 **tablespoons all-purpose flour**
½ **teaspoon caraway seed**
¼ **teaspoon dry mustard**
1 **cup shredded American cheese (4 ounces)**

Thaw spinach and drain (see photo 1). Cut bread into ½-inch cubes. In a 10-inch skillet melt margarine or butter. Add bread and toss to coat (see photo 2). Continue tossing till bread is toasted. Remove bread from skillet; set aside.

In the same skillet break ground pork or beef apart with a wooden spoon; add onion and cook till meat is brown and onion is tender (see photo 3). Drain off fat.

Meanwhile, stir together milk, flour, caraway seed, mustard, dash *salt,* and dash *pepper.* Add milk mixture to meat. Cook and stir till thickened and bubbly. Add cheese; cook and stir till cheese is melted. Stir in spinach. Simmer, covered, for 5 to 10 minutes or till heated through. Spoon mixture into a serving dish and sprinkle bread cubes around the edge (see photo 4). Garnish with celery leaves, if desired. Serves 4.

**2** Add the bread cubes to melted margarine in a skillet. Use a wooden spoon to toss the cubes till all sides are evenly toasted. Remove the cubes; set them aside.

**1** Drain the thawed spinach thoroughly, or the creamed mixture will be too thin. To remove as much liquid as possible from the spinach, use the back of a wooden spoon to press the spinach against the side of the colander.

**3** In the same skillet, break up the ground meat with the same wooden spoon till crumbly. Add the onion, then continue cooking till the meat is brown and the onion is tender.

**4** After spooning the meat mixture into a serving dish, sprinkle the toasted bread cubes on top. Arrange the bread in a wreath around the edge so you can still see the spinach-meat mixture.

# Timetable

**4** hrs. before
- Prepare the vegetables and shake the ingredients for the dressing together for Garden Marinade, as shown. Combine the salad ingredients, then cover and chill. Remember to stir the salad occasionally as it chills so the dressing coats all of the vegetables.
- Start thawing the spinach.

**1** hr. before
- Spoon ice cream into serving dishes; place the dishes in the freezer. Make the Strawberry Sauce; set it aside to cool. Set the table.
- Drain the spinach in a colander, as shown. Cube and toast the bread; set it aside. Cook the ground meat mixture.

## Just Before Serving

- Use a slotted spoon to transfer the Garden Marinade to a lettuce-lined serving platter, as shown. Transfer the meat mixture to a serving dish and sprinkle toasted bread cubes around the edge. Garnish with celery leaves.
- To serve the dessert, remove the dishes of ice cream from the freezer and spoon Strawberry Sauce over the ice cream.
- If desired, serve wine with dinner.

# One-Dish Stroganoff

*Now, creamy stroganoff is easier than ever: It's made in one dish. Serve it as a menu alternative to Meat and Spinach Range-Top Casserole.*

    1   pound ground beef *or* ground pork
 2½   cups water
    1   4-ounce can mushroom stems
          and pieces
    2   tablespoons snipped parsley
    1   tablespoon catsup
  ½   teaspoon instant beef bouillon granules
  ¼   teaspoon pepper
    4   ounces medium noodles
    1   8-ounce container sour cream
          dip with French onion
    2   tablespoons all-purpose flour
        Snipped parsley (optional)

In a 3-quart saucepan cook beef or pork until it's brown. Drain off fat. Stir in water, *undrained* mushrooms, parsley, catsup, bouillon granules, and pepper. Stir in *uncooked* noodles. Bring to boiling. Reduce the heat, then simmer, covered, for 15 to 20 minutes or till the noodles are tender; stir occasionally.

Stir together dip and flour, then stir into meat mixture in saucepan. Cook and stir till thickened and bubbly, then cook and stir for 1 minute more. Sprinkle with parsley, if desired. Makes 4 servings.

# Strawberry Sauce

*Serve the warm sauce over scoops of ice cream.*

    1   12-ounce jar strawberry jam *or*
          preserves (1 cup)
  ¼   cup cranberry juice cocktail
    1   teaspoon margarine *or* butter
  ¼   teaspoon finely shredded orange
          *or* lemon peel

In a small saucepan combine strawberry jam or preserves, cranberry juice, margarine or butter,

and orange or lemon peel. Heat through till jam is melted. Cool slightly before serving over ice cream. Cover and chill leftover sauce in the refrigerator. To reheat sauce, cook and stir over low heat till heated through. Makes 1¼ cups.

**Microwave Directions:** In a 2-cup glass measure combine all ingredients. Micro-cook on 100% power (HIGH) for 2 minutes, stirring twice. To reheat sauce, cook on 100% power (HIGH) for 1 minute or till heated through.

# Garden Marinade

*Turn fresh vegetables into an attractive, make-ahead salad. (Pictured on page 18.)*

    2   small tomatoes, cut into wedges
    1   medium green pepper, cut into rings
  ½   of a medium cucumber, thinly sliced
  ½   of a medium red *or* white onion,
          sliced and separated into rings
  ¼   cup vinegar
    2   tablespoons salad oil
  ½   teaspoon sugar
  ½   teaspoon dried basil, crushed
        Dash salt
        Dash pepper
        Lettuce leaves (optional)

In a large mixing bowl combine tomatoes, green pepper, cucumber, and red or white onion.

In a screw-top jar combine vinegar, oil, sugar, basil, salt, and pepper. Cover and shake well to mix. Pour over vegetables; toss to coat. Cover and chill in the refrigerator for 4 hours, tossing occasionally.

Line a serving plate with lettuce, if desired. Using a slotted spoon, transfer vegetable mixture to the plate. Makes 4 servings.

# Meat Plus Rice

Get six servings from a four-serving pound of ground beef. How? Stretch the meat with rice—not just any rice, but a make-your-own rice mix that's packed with flavor.

The rice mix makes plenty; you'll have extra portions to add pizzazz to other budget-conscious meals, too.

## Menu

- Mini Loaves with Beer-Cheese Sauce*
- Sliced tomatoes on lettuce
- Buttermilk Egg Braid*
- Sherbet and cookies
- Milk

*see pages 26–29*

*Mini Loaves with Beer-Cheese Sauce*

# Savory Rice Mix

3 cups medium grain rice
3 tablespoons dried parsley flakes
5 teaspoons instant beef *or* chicken
 bouillon granules
1 tablespoon minced dried onion
½ teaspoon garlic powder

In a bag or storage container combine rice, parsley, bouillon granules, onion, and garlic powder. Seal tightly. Store on the shelf for up to 6 months. Makes 3 cups mix.

**To prepare rice mix for a side dish:** Shake container to distribute ingredients (see photo 1). In a saucepan combine 1 cup *Savory Rice Mix* and 2 cups *water.* Bring to boiling. Reduce the heat, then simmer, covered, for 15 minutes; do not lift cover. Remove from the heat. Let stand, covered, for 10 minutes. Fluff with a fork. Makes 3 cups.

# Mini Loaves with Beer-Cheese Sauce

⅔ cup water
⅓ cup Savory Rice Mix
1 beaten egg
1 11-ounce can condensed cheddar
 cheese soup
1 pound ground beef
⅓ cup beer *or* apple juice
3 cups shredded zucchini
 (about 2 medium zucchini)

In a small saucepan stir together water and rice mix. Bring to boiling. Reduce the heat, then simmer, covered, for 15 minutes; do not lift the cover. Remove from the heat. Let stand, covered, for 10 minutes. Fluff rice with a fork. Cool slightly.

In a bowl combine egg and ¼ *cup* of the soup. Stir in rice. Add beef; mix well (see photo 2). Shape into 6 loaves (see photo 3). Place in an 8x8x2-inch baking pan. Bake in a 350° oven for 30 to 35 minutes or till done.

Meanwhile, make the sauce. In a saucepan combine the remaining soup and beer or apple juice. Cook and stir till smooth and heated through. Steam zucchini for 2 to 3 minutes or till tender (see photo 4). Place zucchini on a serving platter; arrange the meat loaves atop. Spoon sauce over meat. Garnish with cherry tomatoes, if desired. Makes 6 servings.

**1** Shake rice mix before measuring the desired amount. This redistributes ingredients that may have settled during storage. Our tasty rice mixture has other uses, too: Serve it as a side dish with pork chops or chicken.

**2** Add the beef to the liquid and rice mixture. Then, mix lightly but thoroughly—too much handling causes meat loaves to have a compact texture. You may find that using your hands to thoroughly combine the mixture is easier than using a spoon for mixing.

**3** Gently shape about ½ cup of the meat into a small loaf measuring 3½x2 inches. Place the meat in a baking pan. Repeat with the remaining meat mixture, making a total of six mini loaves.

**4** Place the shredded zucchini in a steamer basket. Set the basket over boiling water in a saucepan. Cover the pan and steam the zucchini just till tender.

# Timetable

**3¼** hrs. before
- Prepare the bread; during rising time, make the rice mix, as shown. (If you're short on time, bake the bread the day before.) Cook the rice for the mini loaves; store the rest of the mix. While the bread bakes, prepare and shape the meat; cover and store it in the refrigerator.
- Wash and drain the lettuce; slice the tomatoes. Arrange the tomatoes on a lettuce-lined plate. Cover; chill.

**35** mins. before
- Place the meat loaves in the oven. While the meat bakes, scoop sherbet into dessert dishes; place the dishes in the freezer so the sherbet stays frosty till serving time. Wash and coarsely shred the zucchini, as shown, then prepare Beer-Cheese Sauce.
- Set the table. Pour milk; slice the bread and place it in a basket. Steam the zucchini and drain well.

**At Serving Time**
- Arrange the meat loaves on a bed of steamed zucchini placed on a serving platter. Spoon on the Beef-Cheese Sauce.
- To serve the dessert, remove the sherbet from the freezer and garnish each serving with a cookie.

# Buttermilk Egg Braid

*Shorten preparation time by using quick-rise yeast.*

5½  to 6 cups all-purpose flour
2  packages active dry yeast
1½  cups buttermilk *or* sour milk
¼  cup margarine *or* butter
¼  cup sugar
2  teaspoons salt
3  eggs
1  egg yolk
1  tablespoon water

In a large mixer bowl combine *2 cups* of flour and yeast. In a saucepan heat buttermilk, margarine or butter, sugar, and salt just till warm (115° to 120°); stir constantly. Add to flour mixture with the 3 eggs. Beat with an electric mixer on low speed for 30 seconds, scraping sides of the bowl constantly. Beat for 3 minutes at high speed. Using a spoon, stir in as much of remaining flour as you can.

Turn dough out onto a lightly floured surface. Knead in enough of the remaining flour to make a moderately soft dough that is smooth and elastic (5 to 8 minutes). Shape into a ball. Place in a lightly greased bowl; turn once to grease surface. Cover and let dough rise in a warm place till double (45 to 60 minutes).

Punch down, then divide dough in half. Cover; let rest for 10 minutes. Divide each half of dough into thirds; shape each into a 16-inch rope. Line up 3 ropes, 1 inch apart, on a greased baking sheet. Begin in the middle of the ropes and work toward the ends to avoid stretching dough. For half of loaf, alternately bring 1 of the outside ropes over the middle rope. Continue to braid loosely so dough has room to expand. Pinch end and tuck under the braid. Repeat braiding for other half of loaf, except alternately bring outside ropes under the middle rope. Cover; let rise for 20 to 30 minutes or till nearly double. Combine egg yolk and water; brush over loaves. Bake in a 375° oven for 15 minutes; cover with foil and bake for 10 minutes more. Cool on wire racks. Makes 2.

## Rice Cooking At Its Best

Whether it's the Savory Rice Mix or plain rice, make sure the rice you fix is tender and fluffy by following these tips:

● Use only the amount of water called for. Draining off the excess water removes valuable nutrients.
● Prevent rice from undercooking or burning by covering the pan with a tight-fitting lid. Remember to keep the cooking heat low.
● Test rice for doneness by pinching a grain between your thumb and forefinger. If there's no hard core, the rice is done.
● Leftover rice is no problem. Just chill it in the refrigerator for up to four days. To reheat it on the range top, add about 2 tablespoons water for each cup of cooked rice. Then, cover and simmer till the rice is heated.

To reheat rice in your microwave oven, place 1 cup of chilled rice in a nonmetal bowl. Cover the bowl with vented clear plastic wrap. Micro-cook on 100% power (HIGH) about 1 minute or till heated through. Stir the rice gently with a fork to fluff.
● For variety, add color to plain cooked rice by adding cooked mixed vegetables or peas.

# Souper Supper

For a good all-around money-saving meal, sit yourself down to not just any soup . . . but *this* wholesome bowl of soup. We've started off our hearty concoction with beef shank crosscuts, then added dried beans and peas to help boost the protein content yet keep down the cost.

## Menu

- Beef and Bean Soup*
- Corn Sticks* with Honey Spread*
- Zucchini sticks, radishes
- Tapioca pudding
- Hot cocoa

*see pages 32–35*

*Beef and Bean Soup*

# Beef and Bean Soup

**1** cup combination of dry garbanzo beans, navy beans, pinto beans, kidney beans, lima beans, *or* whole *or* split peas
**4** cups water
**1** pound beef shank crosscuts
**1** tablespoon cooking oil
**6** cups water
**1** cup chopped onion
**1** cup chopped celery
**⅓** cup wheat berries *or* pearl barley
**1** tablespoon instant beef bouillon granules
**1½** teaspoons dried basil, crushed
**2** bay leaves
**1** teaspoon salt
**¼** teaspoon pepper
**1** 16-ounce can tomatoes, cut up

Select desired beans and/or peas (see photo 1). In a Dutch oven combine 4 cups water and beans (peas do not need to be soaked). Bring to boiling. Reduce the heat, then simmer, covered, for 2 minutes. Remove from the heat. Cover and let stand for 1 hour. (*Or*, soak beans—in the water overnight in a covered pan.) Drain and rinse beans.

In a Dutch oven quickly brown beef in hot oil (see photo 2) for 2 to 3 minutes on each side. Drain off fat. Combine beef, drained beans, and remaining ingredients *except* tomatoes. Bring to boiling. Reduce the heat, then simmer, covered, for 1½ hours. Skim off fat. Remove meat.

When beef is cool enough to handle, remove meat from bones; coarsely chop meat (see photo 3). Discard bones. Remove and discard bay leaves. Return meat to the Dutch oven. Add *undrained* tomatoes. Cover and simmer for 30 minutes more or till meat and beans are tender. Makes 6 servings.

*Red kidney beans*

*Green split peas*

**1** Select the beans or peas you want to use from those listed in the recipe. (Some of them are pictured above.) Use a variety of beans and peas for a more colorful soup, or use just a couple of kinds of beans.

Yellow split peas

Garbanzo beans

Pinto beans

Lima beans

## Crockery Cooker Method

**2** Brown the beef quickly on both sides in hot cooking oil over medium-high heat. Use tongs to turn the meat pieces. Browning the meat enhances the flavor of the soup stock.

**3** After cooking the meat, remove it; set it aside to cool slightly. Then, remove the meat from the bones and cut the meat into small pieces.

Prepare the beans and meat. In an electric crockery cooker combine beans, meat, and remaining ingredients, including tomatoes. Cover; cook on a low-heat setting for 10 to 12 hours. Skim off fat. Remove the meat and bay leaves. Chop meat; add it to the soup.

# Timetable

### 3½ hrs. before
- Choose the desired dried beans or peas for the soup. Whatever you have on hand will make a delicious-tasting soup. Combine the beans and water, then simmer and let stand. The standing time is needed to soak the beans before cooking.
- Meanwhile, cook the pudding (or prepare a mix if you choose). Chill till dessert time.

### 2 hrs. before
- Brown the meat, as shown, then add the remaining ingredients, *except* for the tomatoes. Simmer for 1½ hours or till the meat is tender.
- While the soup is cooking, clean and cut up the zucchini and radishes. Place the relishes in a dish; cover and chill them till serving time.

### 30 mins. before
- Prepare the batter for Corn Sticks and spoon it into corn stick pans, as shown. Bake till golden brown. While the bread bakes, remove the meat and bones from the soup and cut off the meat. Return the cut-up meat and tomatoes to the soup, then heat through.
- Set the table and prepare the cocoa.

### Just Before Serving
- Shred lemon peel for Honey Spread, as shown, then beat the butter mixture together.
- Spoon the pudding into serving dishes and top with small fresh fruit pieces, drained canned fruit, shredded orange peel, or nutmeg, if desired.
- Arrange the warm corn sticks in a basket; serve with Honey Spread. Ladle the soup into bowls and pour the cocoa. Top the cocoa with marshmallows, if desired.

# Corn Sticks

*A quick bread that looks like miniature ears of corn. (Pictured on page 31.)*

1   **cup all-purpose flour**
¾   **cup yellow cornmeal**
¼   **cup sugar**
1   **tablespoon baking powder**
½   **teaspoon salt**
2   **beaten eggs**
¾   **cup milk**
3   **tablespoons cooking oil**

In a bowl stir together flour, cornmeal, sugar, baking powder, and salt. Add eggs, milk, and oil. Stir just till smooth (do not overmix). Spoon batter into greased corn stick pans, filling pans ⅔ full. Bake in a 425° oven for 12 to 15 minutes or till done. Serve warm with Honey Spread, if desired. Makes 14 sticks.

**Corn Bread:** Prepare batter as above. Turn batter into a greased 8x8x2-inch baking pan. Bake in a 425° oven for 18 to 20 minutes or till done. Serve warm. Makes 8 servings.

# Double Apple-Corn Muffins

*If you're looking for a fruity alternative to corn sticks or corn bread, give these out-of-the-ordinary muffins a try!*

1   **cup all-purpose flour**
1   **cup yellow cornmeal**
¼   **cup sugar**
1   **tablespoon baking powder**
½   **teaspoon salt**
2   **eggs**
⅔   **cup applesauce**
½   **cup milk**
¼   **cup cooking oil**
1   **large apple, peeled and finely chopped**

In a mixing bowl stir together flour, cornmeal, sugar, baking powder, and salt; set aside. In a separate bowl beat eggs slightly. Stir in applesauce, milk, and oil.

Stir liquid mixture into dry ingredients just till moistened. Stir in chopped apple till combined. Spoon batter into greased muffin pans, filling pans ⅔ full. Bake in a 425° oven for 15 to 20 minutes. Makes 14 to 16 muffins.

# Honey Spread

*This spread adds both sweetness and richness to your breads all in one mixture. (Pictured on page 31.)*

½   **cup margarine *or* butter, softened**
¼   **teaspoon finely shredded lemon peel**
¼   **cup honey**

In a small mixer bowl combine softened margarine or butter and lemon peel. Gradually add honey, beating with an electric mixer on high speed till fluffy. Store in a covered container in the refrigerator (let spread made with butter stand at room temperature for 1 hour before serving). Makes about ⅔ cup.

# Peanut-Honey Spread

*Add a peanutty punch to Corn Sticks by topping them with Peanut-Honey Spread instead of Honey Spread.*

½   **cup peanut butter**
¼   **cup margarine *or* butter, softened**
¼   **cup toasted wheat germ**
¼   **teaspoon ground cinnamon**
3   **tablespoons honey**

In a small mixer bowl beat together peanut butter, margarine or butter, wheat germ, and cinnamon. Gradually add honey, beating with an electric mixer on high speed till fluffy. Store in a covered container in the refrigerator. Makes about 1 cup.

# Make-Ahead Brunch

Glamorizing leftovers may seem an impossible task, but we've done just that.

Our menu transforms leftover cooked chicken, turkey, or ham into a brunch special enough for company. We've even planned the menu so you can make most of it ahead.

## Menu

- Country Strata*
- Fruit Toss*
- Celery brushes and carrot curls
- Sweet and Sassy Sipper*
- Coffee

*see pages 38-41*

*Country Strata*

# Country Strata

4  slices rye, whole wheat, *or*
   pumpernickel bread
½  cup chopped onion
½  cup chopped green pepper
2  tablespoons margarine *or* butter
1  cup chopped cooked chicken, turkey,
   *or* diced fully cooked ham
1  4-ounce can mushroom stems and
   pieces, drained
1  cup shredded American cheese
4  beaten eggs
1½ cups milk
½  teaspoon dried thyme, crushed
¼  teaspoon pepper

Cut bread slices into 4 triangles. Arrange *half* of the bread triangles in an 8x8x2-inch baking dish (see photo 1). In a small saucepan cook onion and green pepper in hot margarine or butter till tender but not brown. Stir in chicken, turkey, or ham, and mushrooms. Spoon mixture over bread (see photo 2). Top with cheese. Arrange remaining bread on top of cheese (see photo 3). In a bowl stir together eggs, milk, thyme, and pepper. Pour over layered strata (see photo 4). Cover; chill in the refrigerator for 3 to 24 hours.

Bake, uncovered, in a 325° oven about 50 minutes or till a knife inserted near the center comes out clean (see photo 5). Let stand for 10 minutes. Garnish each serving with carrot curls and celery brushes, if desired. Makes 4 servings.

**1** Cut the bread into triangles. Arrange half of the triangles in the bottom of the baking dish, moving the bread around to fit the dish.

**2** Spoon the meat-vegetable layer over the bread, spreading the mixture evenly. Sprinkle on the cheese.

**3** Place the remaining bread triangles on top of the cheese layer. Arrange the pieces so that they fit in an even layer.

**4** Combine the egg, milk, and seasonings, then pour over the layered mixture. Cover and place in the refrigerator for 3 to 24 hours, so the bread can absorb the egg-milk mixture.

**5** To test the baked strata for doneness, insert a knife near the center of the strata mixture. When the food is done, the knife should come out clean, as shown.

# Timetable

**1** day before
- Assemble the strata; cover it with clear plastic wrap to keep it from drying out during chilling.
- Wash celery and carrots. Prepare celery brushes and carrot curls, as shown. (To make celery brushes, make several cuts in celery sticks from both ends almost to the middle.) Place the vegetables in a bowl of icy water; cover and chill.

**2** hrs. before
- Make Sweet and Sassy Sipper by stirring all of the ingredients together in a serving pitcher. Chill.
- Peel and section oranges for the salad, as shown. Prepare the dressing. Combine the fruit with the dressing; cover and chill. Set the table buffet style.

**1** hr. before
- Remove the strata from the refrigerator and remove the covering. Bake.
- Wash a lemon or lime; use a zester to remove the peel in thin strips, as shown. Tie the strips into loose knots; these garnishes will add a special look to the Sweet and Sassy Sipper. Cover the citrus garnishes; set them aside.

**10** mins. before
- Brew the coffee. Test the strata for doneness by inserting a knife near the center, as shown. Let it stand for 10 minutes so it's easier to serve.
- Spoon the salad into lettuce cups. Pour the cold beverage into glasses; add the citrus peel garnish to the drinks.
- Drain the celery brushes and carrot curls. Cut the strata into serving pieces. Garnish the strata with the celery brushes and carrot curls, if desired. Or, serve celery brushes and carrot curls as relishes.

# Reuben-Style Strata

*A layered dish that will remind you of a hot reuben sandwich. Prepare it for brunch as a substitute for Country Strata.*

4  slices rye *or* white bread
⅓  cup well-drained sauerkraut, snipped
½  teaspoon caraway seed
½  pound cooked Polish sausage *or* bratwurst, thinly sliced
¼  cup sliced green onion
4  ounces thinly sliced mozzarella cheese
4  beaten eggs
2  cups milk
1  tablespoon all-purpose flour

Diagonally halve bread slices to make 8 triangles. Arrange *half* of the bread triangles in an 8x8x2-inch baking dish (see photo 1, page 38). In a small mixing bowl stir together sauerkraut and caraway seed; set aside.

In a medium skillet cook sausage and onion for 3 to 4 minutes or till onion is tender but not brown. Drain off fat. Spoon sauerkraut mixture over bread. Top with sausage mixture and cheese slices. Arrange remaining bread on top of cheese (see photo 3, page 38). In a mixing bowl stir together eggs, milk, and flour. Pour over layered strata (see photo 4, page 39). Cover and chill in the refrigerator for 3 to 24 hours.

Bake, uncovered, in a 325° oven for 55 to 60 minutes or till a knife inserted near the center comes out clean (see photo 5, page 39). Let stand for 10 minutes. Makes 4 servings.

# Fruit Toss

2  medium oranges
3  tablespoons salad oil
3  tablespoons honey
2  tablespoons lime *or* lemon juice
¼  teaspoon poppy seed
1  cup seedless green grapes
1  medium apple, cored and chopped
   Lettuce leaves

Peel and section oranges over a small bowl; reserve juice (about 2 tablespoons). For dressing, in a screw-top jar combine reserved orange juice, oil, honey, lime or lemon juice, and poppy seed. Cover and shake till well mixed.

In a large bowl combine orange sections, grapes, and apple. Pour dressing over fruit; toss to coat. Cover and chill for at least 1½ hours, stirring once or twice. With a slotted spoon, divide the fruit mixture among 4 lettuce-lined plates. Pass remaining dressing. Serves 4.

# Sweet and Sassy Sipper

*Apple juice makes it sweet; lemonade makes it sassy. (Pictured on page 36.)*

3  cups apple juice
1  cup water
½  of a 6-ounce can (⅓ cup) frozen lemonade concentrate
   Ice cubes
   Lemon *or* lime peel twists

In a pitcher combine apple juice, water, and lemonade concentrate. Stir gently. Chill. To serve, pour over ice cubes in 4 tall glasses. Garnish each serving with a lemon or lime peel twist. Makes 4 (8-ounce) servings.

**Tomato Sipper:** Prepare Sweet and Sassy Sipper as above, *except* substitute 3 cups *tomato juice* for the apple juice; continue as directed.

# Affordable Beef Dinner

When a standing rib roast is beyond your budget, consider a less costly cut. Select either a beef brisket or chuck pot roast, then cook it in a sassy sauce.

When slowly simmered, these cuts of meat become so-o-o tender they'll practically melt in your mouth.

## Menu

- Sweet and Sour Beef*
- Potato Plate*
- Buttered green beans
- Peach Ice*
- Coffee

*see pages 44–47*

*Sweet and Sour Beef*

# Sweet and Sour Beef

*Choose either a lean beef brisket or a pot roast for this simple, yet sensational, meat dish (see photo 1).*

| | |
|---|---|
| 1 | **2- to 2½-pound fresh beef brisket *or* beef chuck pot roast** |
| 1 | **7½-ounce can tomatoes** |
| 1 | **8-ounce can sauerkraut** |
| ¾ | **cup applesauce** |
| 1 | **tablespoon brown sugar** |
| | **Green pepper rings (optional)** |

Trim excess fat from meat. Cut up tomatoes (see photo 2). In a 10-inch skillet combine *undrained* tomatoes, *undrained* sauerkraut, applesauce, and sugar. Bring to boiling; reduce the heat. Add meat and spoon some tomato mixture over meat (see photo 3).

Simmer, covered, for 2¼ to 2¾ hours or till meat is tender (see photo 4). Spoon some of the tomato-sauerkraut mixture over meat occasionally during cooking. Transfer meat and tomato-sauerkraut mixture to a serving platter. Garnish the meat with green pepper rings, if desired. Makes 6 servings.

**1** Select either beef chuck pot roast (back), a cut of meat with a cross section of the round arm bone, or fresh beef brisket (front), a boneless cut with thick layers of lean meat and little fat.

**2** Make quick work of cutting up canned tomatoes. Use scissors to cut them right in the can. Then, simply add the undrained tomatoes to the meat mixture.

Remember this slick trick each time your recipe calls for cut-up canned tomatoes.

**3** Spoon the tomato-sauerkraut mixture over the meat after it's added to the simmering mixture. Also, during cooking, continue to spoon the tomato-sauerkraut mixture over the meat occasionally to keep it moist.

**4** Test the meat for doneness by piercing it with a fork. The fork should insert and slip out easily when the meat is done. If there is resistance when you insert the fork, it's not done. Continue cooking the meat a little longer, until the fork inserts and slips out easily.

# Timetable

**1** day before
- Prepare Peach Ice, freezing it partially. Beat the mixture till it's light and fluffy, as shown. Return the mixture to the freezer so it has plenty of time to become firm.
- Scrub the potatoes with a vegetable brush. Cook them in boiling water till tender. When the potatoes are cool, place them in the refrigerator to chill.

**3** hrs. before
- Prepare the meat and tomato-sauerkraut mixture, as shown. Simmer, covered, for 2¼ to 2¾ hours or till the meat is tender, spooning the tomato-sauerkraut mixture over the meat occasionally.
- Wash the lettuce or other salad greens and place them in the refrigerator to crisp till serving time. Chill the salad plates, if desired.

**30** mins. before
- While the beans are cooking, slice the potatoes, as shown. Place the lettuce or greens on salad plates, then arrange the potatoes atop. Stir together the salad dressing and drizzle it over the potatoes; sprinkle with parsley. Prepare the coffee and set the table.
- At serving time, transfer the meat and tomato-sauerkraut mixture to a serving platter. Remove Peach Ice from the freezer to soften slightly during dinner.
- Just before serving dessert, scrape the Peach Ice into serving dishes.

# Potato Plate

*Leave the potato skins on for a more attractive salad presentation.*

1   **pound whole tiny new potatoes *or* small potatoes**
     **Shredded lettuce, torn spinach leaves, *or* torn salad greens**
¼  **cup dairy sour cream**
2   **tablespoons creamy French salad dressing**
2   **tablespoons snipped parsley**

Cook new potatoes in boiling salted water for 12 to 15 minutes or till tender. (If using small potatoes, cook for 25 to 30 minutes.) Drain potatoes; cool. Chill. Carefully cut potatoes into ¼-inch-thick slices.

Line 6 individual salad plates with shredded lettuce, spinach, or salad greens. Arrange potato slices on top. For dressing, stir together sour cream and salad dressing; drizzle over salads. Sprinkle with parsley. Makes 6 servings.

## Flavor Vegetables With Herbs

Enhance the flavor of vegetables with herbs. Because such small amounts are needed, this is an inexpensive way to perk up the flavor of ordinary foods. Herbs that go well with vegetables include dill, basil, caraway, marjoram, oregano, and savory.

For four servings, start by adding ¼ teaspoon of a crushed dried herb. If you prefer fresh herbs, start with ¾ teaspoon of a fresh snipped herb. Enough flavor? Taste before adding more.

# Peach Ice

*Tangy and refreshing—it's a peachy way to end a meal.*

1   **29-ounce can peach slices**
2   **tablespoons frozen orange juice concentrate**
¼  **teaspoon ground ginger**
     **Dash ground nutmeg**
1   **teaspoon unflavored gelatin**

Drain peaches, reserving ½ cup syrup. In a blender container place peaches, orange juice concentrate, ginger, and nutmeg. Cover and blend till smooth.

In a small saucepan sprinkle gelatin over reserved syrup; let stand for 1 minute. Stir over low heat till gelatin is dissolved. Add to peach mixture. Cover and blend thoroughly.

Pour mixture into an 8x8x2-inch pan. Cover and freeze about 2 hours or till mixture is partially frozen.

Transfer mixture to a chilled mixer bowl. Beat with an electric mixer till light and fluffy. Return to the pan. Freeze overnight or till firm. Let stand about 15 minutes before serving. Scrape to serve. Makes 2½ to 3 cups mixture.

# Meatless Supper

Forget meat for a change! Instead, choose an inexpensive alternative.

Need an idea? We stuffed flour tortilla bundles with a spicy refried bean mixture, tomato, and cheese. It's a great "no meat" solution.

## Menu

- South-of-the-Border Bundles*
- Relish tray
- Chocolate-Macaroon Cupcakes*
- Iced tea

*see pages 50–53

*South-of-the-Border Bundles*

# South-of-the-Border Bundles

**6** **10-inch flour tortillas**
**6** **ounces cheddar cheese** *or* **American cheese**
**1** **16-ounce can refried beans**
**½** **cup sliced green onions**
**1** **4-ounce can green chili peppers, rinsed, seeded, and chopped**
**1** **teaspoon chili powder**
**1** **large tomato, cored and chopped**
**Taco sauce (optional)**
**Sliced green onion**

Wrap tortillas tightly in foil (see photo 1). Heat in a 350° oven for 10 minutes. Meanwhile, cut cheese into 6 sticks (see photo 2). In a mixing bowl stir together beans, ½ cup green onions, chili peppers, and chili powder.

Remove *1* tortilla from foil. Spread tortilla with about *½ cup* bean mixture to within 2 inches of the edge (see photo 3). Top with *1 tablespoon* chopped tomato. Place *1* cheese stick in center of tortilla (see photo 4). Fold in 2 sides; roll up (see photo 5). Place on a greased baking sheet. Repeat with remaining tortillas.

Bake in a 350° oven for 15 to 20 minutes or till heated through. To serve, spoon taco sauce atop bundles, if desired. Sprinkle with green onion. Makes 6 servings.

**1** To make the tortillas pliable and easier to work with, wrap them tightly in foil so they don't dry out, then heat them in the oven. Keep the rest of the tortillas covered while you're working with one.

**2** Cut the cheese into sticks measuring 2x1x¾ inches. The sticks need to be approximately this size so they will fit neatly into the bundles.

**3** Working quickly with one heated tortilla at a time, spread some bean mixture on each. Leave a 2-inch border around the edge so the mixture won't spill out of the tortilla.

**4** Using about 1 tablespoon of chopped tomato, sprinkle the tomato evenly over the bean-spread tortilla. Then, place a cheese stick in the center of the tortilla, as shown.

**5** Fold in two sides of the tortilla, envelope fashion. Roll up the tortilla so the beans and cheese are enclosed. As each tortilla is rolled up, place it on a greased baking sheet.

# Timetable

**4** hrs. before
- Make the Chocolate-Macaroon Cupcakes, spooning the macaroon mixture atop the batter in each cup, as shown. Bake till done. Transfer the cupcakes to a wire rack. When the cupcakes cool, cover the cupcakes, and store them.

**3** hrs. before
- Select vegetables for the relish tray: carrots, celery, cucumber, broccoli, cauliflower, zucchini, radishes, or any vegetables you have on hand. Wash the vegetables and cut them into easy-to-eat pieces. Put the vegetables in a bowl of ice water, as shown; chill in the refrigerator to crisp.
- Prepare the iced tea.

**1** hr. before
- Prepare South-of-the-Border Bundles, as shown. Bake for 15 to 20 minutes or till they're heated through. Set the table while the bundles bake.

## At Serving Time
- Arrange the cupcakes on one plate and the drained vegetable relishes on another plate. Place a baked tortilla bundle on each dinner plate, then top with taco sauce. Sprinkle each serving with sliced green onion, as shown.
- Pour the tea over ice cubes.

# Zucchini-Cheese Frittata

*A tasty substitute for South-of-the-Border Bundles!*

| | |
|---|---|
| 1 | tablespoon margarine *or* butter |
| 1 | tablespoon cornstarch |
| 1 | cup milk |
| ½ | cup shredded process Swiss cheese (2 ounces) |
| 2 | tablespoons finely shredded carrot |
| 2 | small zucchini, cut into ¼-inch slices (about 1⅓ cups) |
| ½ | cup chopped onion |
| 1 | tablespoon cooking oil |
| 10 | beaten eggs |
| ⅓ | cup milk |
| ⅓ | cup grated Parmesan cheese |
| ½ | teaspoon dried basil, rosemary, *or* thyme, crushed |
| ¼ | teaspoon salt |

For sauce, in a small saucepan melt margarine or butter. Stir in cornstarch. Add 1 cup milk. Cook and stir till thickened and bubbly, then cook and stir for 2 minutes more. Stir in Swiss cheese till melted. Stir in carrot. Set sauce aside and keep warm.

In a 10-inch ovenproof skillet cook zucchini and onion in hot oil about 5 minutes or just till vegetables are tender. Meanwhile, in a mixing bowl stir together eggs, ⅓ cup milk, Parmesan cheese, basil, rosemary or thyme, and salt.

Pour egg mixture into the skillet. Cook over medium-low heat, lifting mixture occasionally to allow uncooked portion to flow underneath. Cook for 4 to 5 minutes or till mixture is nearly set. Place skillet under the broiler, 4 to 5 inches from the heat. Broil about 2 minutes or till eggs are set. Cut into wedges. Serve with sauce. Makes 6 servings.

# Chocolate-Macaroon Cupcakes

*Coconut-capped cupcakes. (Pictured on page 48.)*

| | |
|---|---|
| 1 | egg white |
| ¼ | teaspoon vanilla |
| 3 | tablespoons sugar |
| ⅓ | cup flaked coconut |
| 1 | package 1-layer-size chocolate cake mix |

In a small bowl beat egg white and vanilla till soft peaks form (tips curl). Gradually add sugar, beating till stiff peaks form (tips stand straight). Fold in coconut. Prepare cake mix according to package directions.

Line 12 muffin cups with paper bake cups. Fill about ⅔ full with batter. Drop about 1 rounded tablespoon of coconut mixture onto batter in each muffin cup. Bake in a 350° oven about 20 minutes or till done. Let cool. Makes 12.

# Peanutty Topper

*An easy, make-ahead ice cream or fruit topper alternative to the Chocolate-Macaroon Cupcakes.*

| | |
|---|---|
| ½ | cup quick-cooking rolled oats |
| ½ | cup flaked coconut |
| 2 | tablespoons brown sugar |
| 2 | tablespoons coarsely chopped peanuts |
| ¼ | cup peanut butter |

In a small mixing bowl stir together oats, coconut, sugar, and peanuts. Stir in peanut butter. Spread evenly in an 8x8x2-inch baking pan.

Bake in a 350° oven about 15 minutes or till light brown. Cool slightly; crumble. Serve over fruit, ice cream, or pudding. Store on the shelf in a tightly covered container for up to 1 month. Makes about 1½ cups.

# Favorite Fish Dinner

Waste not, want not! Frozen block fish is a great buy because there's no waste: all of the fish is used. With no bones or fat to bother with, you can eat every morsel.

After sampling these delicate fish fillets, you'll want to prepare this sea fare often.

## Menu

- Oriental Soup*

- Lemony Fish Dinner*

- Oven-Cooked Rice*

- Almond Tea Cakes*

- Hot tea

*see pages 56–59

*Lemony Fish Dinner*

# Lemony Fish Dinner

**1  16-ounce package frozen fish fillets**
**1  10-ounce package frozen cut broccoli**
**½  cup water**
**1  cup sliced yellow summer squash**
    *or* **zucchini**
**½  cup cold water**
**¾  teaspoon finely shredded lemon peel**
**2  tablespoons lemon juice**
**4  teaspoons cornstarch**
**4  teaspoons honey**
**1  tablespoon soy sauce**

Thaw fish for 30 minutes. Cut partially thawed fish into 5 pieces (see photo 1). Place fish in a greased shallow baking pan. Bake, uncovered, in a 350° oven for 30 to 35 minutes or till fish flakes easily with a fork.

Meanwhile, in a medium saucepan bring broccoli and ½ cup water to boiling. Separate broccoli with a fork (see photo 2). Stir in sliced yellow squash or zucchini. Cover and cook for 5 to 7 minutes or till vegetables are crisp-tender (see photo 3). Drain.

Meanwhile, make sauce. In a small saucepan combine ½ cup cold water, lemon peel and juice, cornstarch, honey, and soy sauce. Cook and stir till thickened and bubbly, then cook and stir for 2 minutes more. Reserve ¼ cup of sauce; set aside. Add vegetables to sauce in pan; toss gently. Cook till heated through. Place vegetable mixture on a serving platter. Arrange fish on top of vegetable mixture (see photo 4). Spoon reserved sauce over fish. Serves 5.

**1** Let the frozen fish stand at room temperature for 20 minutes so you can cut the block into serving portions. With a large knife, cut the fish into five equal pieces.

**2** After the water boils, use a fork to separate the frozen broccoli pieces to ensure that they cook evenly.

**3** When the broccoli is separated, add the sliced squash. Cover and cook till the vegetables are crisp-tender. To test for doneness, stick a fork into several of the squash slices and broccoli pieces. The squash should be slightly crisp and the broccoli should be crisp-tender.

**4** To serve the fish and vegetable mixture, toss some of the sauce with the cooked, drained vegetables and place them on the serving plate.

Using a spatula, arrange the cooked fish on top of the vegetable mixture, then spoon the remaining sauce over the fish.

# Timetable

| | | |
|---|---|---|
| **2½** hrs. before | ● Start off dinner preparations with the Almond Tea Cakes (cookies). Sprinkle them with the sugar-spice mixture, as shown, then bake till the edges are golden. Immediately transfer the baked cookies to a wire rack for cooling. These cookies freeze well and can be made up to several months in advance. |  |
| **1¼** hrs. before | ● Set the fish out to thaw. It will take about 20 minutes for the fish to thaw enough so it can be cut. Divide the partially thawed fish into 5 equal portions, as shown.<br>● While the fish thaws, set the table. Cut up the vegetables for the fish sauce and soup. |  |
| **45** mins. before | ● Prepare Oven Rice. Place the fish in the oven with the rice. Near the end of the baking time, continue soup preparations, cook the vegetables, and prepare tea. Measure the ingredients for the fish sauce. Test the rice for doneness by squeezing a grain of rice between your fingers, as shown. If no hard core is present, it's cooked. |  |
| **At Serving Time** | ● Serve the soup. Prepare the sauce for the fish. Spoon the rice into a serving bowl. Place the vegetables on a serving platter, then arrange the fish atop, as shown. Pour the remaining sauce over the fish. Serve tea with the fish and rice.<br>● Before serving dessert, place Almond Tea Cakes on a plate or in a basket. Serve with more tea. |  |

# Oriental Soup

*Start off dinner with this light appetizer soup. (Pictured on page 55.)*

2¼　cups water
　1　tablespoon instant beef bouillon
　　　granules
　1　tablespoon white wine vinegar *or*
　　　rice wine vinegar
　1　tablespoon soy sauce
　1　cup thinly bias-sliced celery
　¾　cup thinly sliced carrots
　3　green onions

In a saucepan combine water, bouillon granules, wine or rice wine vinegar, and soy sauce. Bring to boiling. Reduce the heat. Add celery and carrots. Simmer, uncovered, for 5 minutes. Bias-slice green onions into 1-inch pieces; add to soup. Simmer for 2 minutes more or till vegetables are crisp-tender. Makes 5 servings.

# Egg Drop Soup

*Try this simple soup as a substitute for Oriental Soup.*

　3　cups water
　1　tablespoon cornstarch
　4　teaspoons instant chicken bouillon
　　　granules
　2　tablespoons thinly sliced green onion
　1　well-beaten egg

In a saucepan gradually stir water into cornstarch; add bouillon granules. Cook and stir till slightly thickened and bubbly. Stir in onion. Cook for 2 minutes more over medium-low heat. Slowly pour in egg; stir once gently to break egg into pieces. Makes 5 servings

# Almond Tea Cakes

*Cookies with a cakelike texture. (Pictured on page 54.)*

　2　teaspoons lemon juice
　½　cup milk
　2　cups all-purpose flour
　1　teaspoon baking powder
　¼　teaspoon baking soda
　½　cup margarine *or* butter
　¾　cup sugar
　1　egg
　½　teaspoon almond extract
　2　tablespoons sugar
　¼　teaspoon ground nutmeg *or* cinnamon

Stir lemon juice into milk. Stir together flour, baking powder, soda, and ¼ teaspoon *salt*. Beat margarine or butter for 30 seconds. Add ¾ cup sugar, beating till fluffy. Add egg and extract; beat well. Add dry ingredients and milk alternately to beaten mixture; beat well after each addition. Drop from a teaspoon 2 inches apart onto an ungreased cookie sheet. Combine 2 tablespoons sugar and spice; sprinkle cookies with mixture. Bake in a 350° oven for 12 to 14 minutes or till edges are golden. Immediately transfer to a wire rack. Makes 42 cookies.

## Oven-Cooked Rice

When you're baking other parts of the meal in the oven, why not cook the rice in the oven, too?

To prepare oven rice, in a 1½-quart casserole stir 1 tablespoon *margarine or butter* into 2¼ cups *boiling water* till melted. Add 1 cup *medium grain rice* and 1 teaspoon *salt*. Cover and bake in a 350° oven about 35 minutes or till the rice is done. Stir the rice with a fork after 15 minutes.

# Weekend Pizza Feast

For a fun twist to weekend activities, try a pizza party. Fresh from the oven and piping hot, this homemade pizza is loaded with rich sauce, crunchy green pepper, and melted cheese. With the self-serve salad bar and make-your-own ice cream cones, you'll have time to enjoy company *and* dinner.

## Menu

- Zesty Pork Pizza*

- Salad Bar:
  Curried Macaroni Salad*
  Tossed salad
  Fruit Fix-Up*

- Soft drinks

- Ice cream cones

*see pages 62–65*

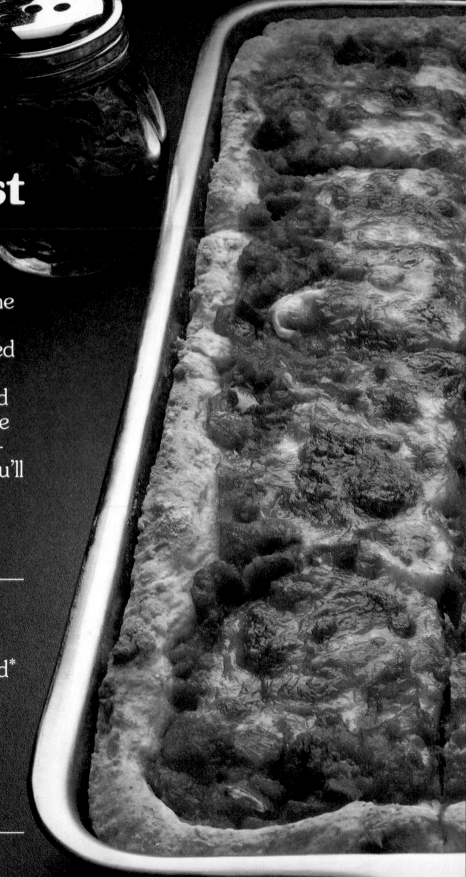

*Zesty Pork Pizza*

# Zesty Pork Pizza

1 **pound ground pork**
½ **cup chopped green pepper *or* canned green chili peppers, rinsed, seeded, and chopped**
1 **small onion, chopped**
1 **15-ounce can pizza sauce**
1½ **teaspoons Italian seasoning, crushed**
2½ **cups packaged biscuit mix**
¼ **cup grated Parmesan cheese**
⅔ **cup cold water**
1 **cup shredded mozzarella, Monterey Jack, *or* cheddar cheese (4 ounces)**

In a medium skillet cook pork, green pepper or chili peppers, and onion till meat is brown and vegetables are tender. Drain off fat (see photo 1). Stir in pizza sauce and Italian seasoning; set the skillet aside.

In a large mixing bowl stir together biscuit mix and Parmesan cheese. Add water. Stir till moistened (see photo 2). Pat dough onto bottom and halfway up the sides of a greased 15x10x1-inch baking pan (see photo 3).

Spoon the pork mixture over dough (see photo 4). Sprinkle pizza with mozzarella, Monterey Jack, or cheddar cheese (see photo 5). Bake in a 425° oven for 20 to 25 minutes or till bubbly. Cut into pieces to serve. Makes 6 servings.

**1** To drain the fat from the cooked meat, transfer the meat to a colander placed over a bowl. Let the meat drain for a few minutes to remove as much fat as possible. Discard the fat.

**2** With a wooden spoon, stir together the dry ingredients and water until completely moistened. Scrape the sides and bottom of the bowl occasionally to combine all of the ingredients.

**3** Using floured or greased fingers, pat the dough from the center out toward the edges and halfway up the sides of the pan, as shown. Pat to the same thickness so the crust bakes evenly.

**4** Spoon the pork mixture onto the dough. With the back of the spoon, spread the mixture out over the pizza, making sure the mixture covers the entire surface of the dough.

**5** Sprinkle the shredded cheese over the pork mixture. The cheese goes on last so it melts down over the meat mixture as the pizza bakes.

# Timetable

**4** hrs. before
- Make Curried Macaroni Salad. Cover and chill for at least 3 hours. Next, make Fruit Fix-Up; cover and chill.
- Wash and drain the lettuce for the tossed salad. Tear the lettuce into a large bowl. Cover the torn greens with a damp paper towel; chill. This keeps the lettuce crisp.

**50** mins. before
- Prepare the pizza crust dough, as shown; pat into a greased baking pan. Spread the cooked pork mixture over the dough, then sprinkle with shredded cheese. Bake the pizza for 20 to 25 minutes or till bubbly.

**30** mins. before
- Serve your family or guests buffet style, so they can help themselves. Set out plates, flatware, and glasses on a kitchen counter or a table. Make cleanup extra-easy by using disposable items.
- Pour your favorite salad dressings into small bowls or pitchers. Place greens in a salad bowl.
- Spoon the Fruit Fix-Up into a lettuce-lined bowl. Set the Curried Macaroni Salad, Fruit Fix-Up, and tossed salad on the table.

**At Serving Time**
- Cut the pizza into pieces. Pour soft drinks into ice-filled glasses.
- At dessert time, ask family or guests to join you in the kitchen and let them make their own ice cream cones.

# Pizza Spuds

*If you like the taste of pizza, you'll want to give Pizza Spuds a try sometime, in place of Zesty Pork Pizza.*

6   **large baking potatoes (6 to 8 ounces each)**
½   **cup chopped green pepper *or* canned green chili peppers, rinsed, seeded, and chopped**
1   **small onion, chopped**
2   **tablespoons water**
1   **8-ounce package frankfurters (5), cut into thin slices**
1   **8-ounce can pizza sauce**
½   **teaspoon dried basil *or* oregano, crushed**
½   **cup shredded mozzarella, Monterey Jack, *or* cheddar cheese (2 ounces)**

Scrub and prick potatoes. Bake in a 425° oven for 40 to 60 minutes. Cut potatoes in half lengthwise and fluff with a fork.

Meanwhile, in a medium saucepan cook green pepper or chili peppers and onion in water till tender; drain. Stir in frankfurters, pizza sauce, and basil or oregano. Cook about 5 minutes or till heated through. Evenly divide sauce among potato halves. Sprinkle with cheese. Serves 6.

**Microwave Directions:** Scrub and prick potatoes. In a countertop microwave oven arrange potatoes on paper towels, leaving at least 1 inch between potatoes. Micro-cook, uncovered, on 100% power (HIGH) for 17 to 19 minutes, turning and rearranging potatoes once. In a nonmetal bowl combine green pepper or chili peppers, onion, and water. Micro-cook, covered, on 100% power (HIGH) for 2 to 3 minutes or till tender; drain. Stir in frankfurters, pizza sauce, and basil or oregano. Micro-cook, uncovered, on 100% power (HIGH) for 4 to 5 minutes or till mixture is heated through. Continue as directed.

# Fruit Fix-Up

*Make this menu super-simple by preparing both Fruit Fix-Up and Curried Macaroni Salad the night before. Just cover and chill till serving time.*

1   **17-ounce can fruit cocktail**
1   **tablespoon frozen orange juice concentrate**
¼   **teaspoon ground cinnamon**
1   **medium apple, cored and thinly sliced**
2   **tablespoons raisins**
    **Lettuce leaves**

Drain fruit cocktail, reserving ¼ cup syrup. For dressing, in a small bowl stir together reserved syrup, orange juice concentrate, and cinnamon. In a medium mixing bowl combine drained fruit cocktail, apple, and raisins. Pour dressing over fruit mixture; toss.

Chill for at least 1 hour, stirring once or twice. Line serving bowl with lettuce leaves. Spoon salad into lettuce-lined bowl. Makes 6 servings.

# Curried Macaroni Salad

1   **cup elbow, corkscrew, *or* medium shell macaroni**
¾   **cup salad dressing *or* mayonnaise**
⅓   **cup milk**
1   **teaspoon curry powder**
1   **teaspoon vinegar**
¼   **teaspoon salt**
    **Dash pepper**
1   **cup shredded carrot**
½   **cup sliced green onion**

Cook macaroni according to package directions; drain. Rinse with cold water. Drain.

In a bowl combine salad dressing or mayonnaise, milk, curry, vinegar, salt, and pepper. Add macaroni, carrot, and onion; toss to coat. Cover and chill for at least 3 hours. Makes 6 servings.

# Bumper Crop Luncheon

Summer brings an abundant supply of fresh fruits and vegetables. When gardens, markets, and roadside stands brim with produce, take advantage of these summer savings with this versatile luncheon.

## Menu

- Summer Stir-Fry*
- Garden Patch Bread*
- Bumper Crop Shortcake*
- Lemonade

*see pages 68-71

*Summer Stir-Fry*

# Summer Stir-Fry

|     |                                                      |
| --- | ---------------------------------------------------- |
| 2   | **pounds chicken breasts and thighs**                |
| ⅔   | **cup orange, pineapple, *or* apple juice**          |
| ¼   | **cup water**                                        |
| 2   | **tablespoons cornstarch**                           |
| 2   | **tablespoons dry white wine *or* dry sherry**       |
| 1   | **teaspoon instant chicken bouillon granules**       |
| 1   | **teaspoon dried basil, crushed, *or* 1 tablespoon snipped fresh basil** |
| 1   | **teaspoon dried marjoram, crushed, *or* 1 tablespoon snipped fresh marjoram** |
| ½   | **teaspoon salt**                                    |
| 2   | **tablespoons cooking oil**                          |
| 3   | **cups Vegetable I (see photo 1)**                   |
| 2   | **cups Vegetable II (see photo 1)**                  |
| 6   | **green onions, bias-sliced into 1-inch pieces**     |
| 2   | **medium tomatoes, cut into wedges**                 |

Skin and bone chicken (see photos 2 and 3). Discard skin and bones. Cut chicken into 1-inch pieces. In a small bowl combine juice, water, cornstarch, wine, bouillon granules, basil, marjoram, and salt; set aside.

Preheat a wok or large skillet over high heat; add *half* of the cooking oil. Stir-fry Vegetable I for 3 minutes. Add Vegetable II; stir-fry for 2 minutes. Add green onions; stir-fry about 1 minute more or till vegetables are crisp-tender (see photo 4). Remove from wok or skillet. Add remaining oil. Stir-fry *half* of the chicken for 2 to 3 minutes or till done. Remove. Repeat with remaining chicken. Return all chicken to wok or skillet. Push chicken from the center of the wok or skillet.

Stir sauce; add to the center of wok or skillet. Cook and stir till thickened and bubbly, then cook and stir for 2 minutes more. Return vegetables and tomatoes to wok. Cover and cook for 1 minute more. Serve immediately. Serves 6.

**1** Select your favorite vegetables for the stir-fry. Choose from bias-sliced carrots, sliced cauliflower flowerets, and/or thinly sliced broccoli to equal 3 cups of Vegetable I. Vegetable II is bias-sliced celery, thinly sliced zucchini, and/or thinly sliced yellow squash.

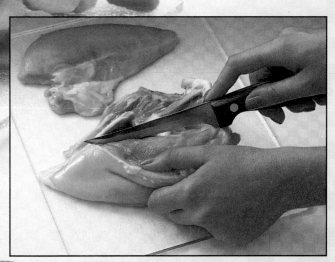

**2** Place the skinned chicken breast on a cutting board, meat side up. Starting at one side of the breastbone, use a sharp knife to cut the meat from the bone. Cut as close to the bone as possible, as shown. Press the knife's flat side against the rib bones and, with a sawing motion, continue cutting. Gently pull the meat away from the rib.

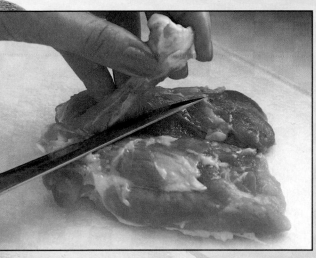

**3** Place the skinned chicken thigh on a cutting board. Using a sharp knife, make a cut down each side of the thigh bone. Pull the meat away from the bone at the two cuts. Lift the bone and carefully cut away the meat, as shown.

**4** Using a spatula or spoon with a long handle, gently lift and turn the food with a folding motion. Keep the food moving so it doesn't burn. If you dont' have a wok, a skillet works just as well.

# Timetable

**4** hrs. before
- Make Garden Patch Bread. Knead the dough until it's moderately smooth and elastic, as shown. Shape the dough into loaves. Bake. After the bread cools, place it in clear plastic bags and store. Or, for longer storage, place the bread in plastic bags and freeze.

**1½** hrs. before
- Prepare Rhubarb-Strawberry or Cherry-Banana Filling, as shown. While the filling cools, make the shortcake dough. Drop the dough into 6 mounds on a greased baking sheet. Bake and cool.
- Bone the chicken pieces. Select the vegetables you are going to use for the stir-fry. Clean and cut the vegetables as directed.

## Just Before Serving
- Place ice cubes in glasses and pour lemonade.
- Heat the wok or skillet. Prepare the stir-fry.
- Before serving dessert, split the individual shortcakes in half horizontally with a serrated knife, as shown. Place the filling on the shortcakes. Dollop with whipped dessert topping.

# Garden Patch Bread

*This delicious whole wheat bread is loaded with garden-fresh cabbage, celery, parsley, and carrot. (Pictured on page 67.)*

1   package active dry yeast
⅓   cup warm water (110° to 115°)
¾   cup coarsely chopped cabbage
1   5-ounce can (⅔ cup) evaporated milk
1   carrot, cut up
¼   cup sliced celery
¼   cup snipped parsley
¼   cup cooking oil
1   egg
2   tablespoons honey
1   teaspoon salt
3   cups whole wheat flour
1   to 1½ cups all-purpose flour

In a large bowl dissolve yeast in warm water. In a blender container or food processor bowl combine cabbage, milk, carrot, celery, parsley, oil, egg, honey, and salt. Cover; blend or process till smooth. Add vegetable mixture to the yeast. Using a spoon, stir in whole wheat flour and as much all-purpose flour as you can. Turn out onto a lightly floured surface.

Knead in enough remaining all-purpose flour to make a moderately stiff dough that is smooth and elastic (6 to 8 minutes). Shape into a ball. Place in a greased bowl; turn dough once. Cover; let the dough rise in a warm place till double (about 1 hour).

Punch down; divide dough in half. Cover; let rest for 10 minutes. Shape into 2 round loaves. Place on a greased baking sheet. Cover; let rise till double (about 30 minutes). Bake in a 350° oven for 20 to 25 minutes or till done. Cool on a wire rack. Makes 2 loaves.

# Bumper Crop Shortcake

**Strawberry-Rhubarb Filling *or* Cherry-Banana Filling**
1   cup all-purpose flour
1   tablespoon sugar
1½   teaspoons baking powder
⅛   teaspoon salt
¼   cup margarine *or* butter
1   beaten egg
¼   cup milk
½   of a 4-ounce container frozen whipped dessert topping, thawed

Prepare your choice of filling. Set aside. In a medium bowl stir together flour, sugar, baking powder, and salt. Cut in margarine or butter till mixture resembles coarse crumbs. Combine egg and milk; add to dry ingredients. Stir just till moistened. Drop into 6 equal mounds on a greased baking sheet. Bake in a 450° oven for 7 to 8 minutes or till done.

Split shortcakes in half horizontally. Spoon about ¼ *cup* filling on the bottom half of each shortcake. Top with remaining halves, then top with remaining filling. Dollop with whipped dessert topping. Makes 6 servings.

**Strawberry-Rhubarb Filling:** In a saucepan combine 1½ cups fresh *rhubarb* cut into 1-inch pieces, ⅓ cup *sugar*, ⅓ cup *water*, and ¼ teaspoon ground *cinnamon*. Bring to boiling; reduce the heat. Simmer about 5 minutes or till rhubarb is tender. Set rhubarb mixture aside. When mixture is lukewarm, stir in 2 cups sliced fresh *strawberries*.

**Cherry-Banana Filling:** In a saucepan combine 2 cups fresh *dark sweet cherries*, pitted and halved; ¼ cup *water*; 2 tablespoons *sugar*; and 2 teaspoons *cornstarch*. Cook and stir till thickened and bubbly, then cook and stir for 2 minutes more. Set aside. When the mixture is lukewarm, stir in 2 *bananas*, sliced; 2 teaspoons *lemon juice*; and ½ teaspoon *vanilla*.

# Harvesttime Dinner

When leaves start to turn color and a brisk chill is in the air, you know fall is just around the corner. What better way to save pennies than to sample the best of autumn's bounty in a delicious dinnertime feast.

## Menu

- Roast Turkey with Corn Bread Stuffing*
- Whipped potatoes
- Pear Waldorf Salad*
- Cranberry Apple Mold*
- Pumpkin pie
- Hot Sippin' Cider*

*see pages 74-77*

*Roast Turkey with Corn Bread Stuffing*

# Roast Turkey

1 **6- to 8-pound fresh *or* frozen turkey**
**Cooking oil *or* melted margarine**

Thaw turkey, if frozen. Rinse turkey and pat dry with paper towels. To stuff turkey, spoon some Corn Bread Stuffing loosely into neck cavity (see photo 2). Pull neck skin over stuffing to back of the bird and fasten securely with a skewer. Lightly spoon the remaining stuffing into the body cavity. Holding turkey by its legs, gently shake the stuffing down; do not pack the stuffing. If turkey has a band of skin across its tail, tuck the legs under band (see photo 3). Twist wing tips under back.

Place the turkey, breast side up, on a rack in a shallow roasting pan. Brush skin with cooking oil or melted margarine. Insert a meat thermometer in the center of inside thigh muscle (see photo 4). Do not add water. Tent turkey with foil (see photo 5).

Roast in a 325° oven for 3 to 3½ hours. Uncover during the last 45 minutes of roasting to let turkey brown. When turkey is done, thermometer should register 180° to 185°F. Remove turkey from oven and let stand for 15 minutes; cover loosely with foil to keep warm. Carve. Serves 8 to 10.

# Corn Bread Stuffing

3 **cups crumbled corn bread**
2 **cups dry bread cubes**
1 **cup chopped celery**
¼ **cup chopped onion**
⅓ **cup margarine *or* butter**
1 **tablespoon sugar**
½ **teaspoon ground sage**
⅓ **to ½ cup water**

In a large bowl combine corn bread and bread cubes. In a skillet or saucepan cook celery and onion in margarine or butter till tender. Stir in sugar and sage; mix well. Add vegetable mixture to corn bread mixture. Toss lightly (see photo 1). Add enough water to moisten; toss gently. Use to stuff a 6- to 8-pound turkey. (*Or,* bake, covered, in an ungreased 1½-quart casserole in a 350° oven for 30 minutes.) Makes 8 servings.

**1** Using a spoon, toss the stuffing mixture together till it's thoroughly combined. The stuffing should be evenly moist. Wait until just before cooking the turkey to stuff it.

**2** Loosely spoon some of the stuffing into the neck cavity, as shown. Spoon the remaining stuffing into the body cavity. If packed too tightly, the stuffing won't be fluffy.

**3** If the turkey has a band of skin across the tail, tuck the legs under it, as shown. If it doesn't, tie the legs together with a piece of string, then tie the legs to the tail to secure.

**4** Insert a meat thermometer into the center of the inside thigh muscle, making sure the bulb doesn't touch the bone. This part of the turkey requires the longest cooking time.

**5** Cover the turkey loosely with foil. Make a tent with the foil, leaving an air space between the bird and the foil, as shown.

# Timetable

**2** days before
- Thaw the frozen turkey in a sink of cool water, as shown. Prepare the pumpkin pie; cover and chill.
- Prepare Cranberry Apple Mold; chill.

**5** hrs. before
- Prepare Corn Bread Stuffing, as shown. Stuff the neck cavity of the turkey, then stuff the body cavity. Insert a meat thermometer into the turkey. Place the turkey in the oven to start roasting.

**1½** hrs. before
- Cut up the pears, as shown. Cut up the celery, grapes, and banana for Pear Waldorf Salad. Sprinkle the fruit with lemon juice. The lemon juice helps prevent the fruit from turning brown.
- Spoon the salad into a serving dish. Cover and chill till serving time.

**45** mins. before
- Remove the foil so the turkey browns as it finishes roasting. Start cooking the potatoes. Check the turkey for doneness. Make the spice bag for Hot Sippin' Cider, as shown.

**At Serving Time**
- Carefully unmold Cranberry Apple Mold onto a serving plate, as shown. Garnish with lettuce leaves, if desired.
- Carve the turkey and transfer it to a serving platter. Whip the potatoes; add margarine, salt, and pepper to taste. While you enjoy dinner, let the Hot Sippin' Cider simmer on your range.
- Just before serving the dessert, pour the cider into mugs or cups. Cut the pie into wedges; dollop each slice with whipped topping, if desired.

# Pear Waldorf Salad

*Sunflower nuts add crunch to this fruity salad. (Pictured on page 72.)*

3 medium pears, cored and chopped
¾ cup sliced celery
¾ cup red *or* green grapes, halved and seeded
1 medium banana, sliced
1 tablespoon lemon juice
1 egg white
½ cup salad dressing *or* mayonnaise
2 tablespoons milk
1 tablespoon sugar
2 tablespoons sunflower nuts

In a large bowl combine pears, celery, grapes, and banana. Sprinkle lemon juice over fruit mixture and toss. In a small bowl use a rotary beater to beat egg white till soft peaks form (tips curl).

For dressing, in a small bowl combine salad dressing or mayonnaise, milk, and sugar. Fold in egg white. Fold dressing into fruit mixture. Cover and chill for up to 1 hour, if desired. Sprinkle with sunflower nuts. Makes 8 servings.

# Cranberry Apple Mold

*The cranberries will "pop," exposing their juicy interior, as they cook. (Pictured on page 73.)*

1¾ cups sugar
1¼ cups water
1 cup applesauce
1 12-ounce package whole cranberries (3 cups)
Lettuce leaves (optional)

In a large saucepan combine sugar, water, and applesauce. Bring to boiling, stirring to dissolve sugar. Boil rapidly for 5 minutes. Add cranberries, then return to boiling. Cook over medium to medium-high heat for 10 to 12 minutes or till a drop gels on a cold plate. Turn mixture into a 4-cup mold. Chill till firm.

Dip mold in warm water for a few seconds to loosen edges. Place a serving plate over mold and invert. Shake gently to unmold. Arrange lettuce leaves around the mold, if desired. Makes 8 servings.

# Hot Sippin' Cider

4 cups apple juice *or* cider
1½ cups unsweetened white grape juice
3 inches stick cinnamon, broken
½ teaspoon whole cloves

In a saucepan combine apple juice and grape juice. Place cinnamon and cloves in cheesecloth and tie. Add to saucepan. Bring to boiling. Reduce the heat. Simmer, covered, for 10 minutes. Discard spices. Makes 8 (5½-ounce) servings.

## Good Gravy!

Use this gravy to accompany the turkey and potatoes. Transfer the turkey to a serving platter; cover with foil. Leaving crusty bits from the turkey in the roasting pan, pour drippings into a large measuring cup. Skim off and reserve fat. Return ¼ *cup* fat to the pan. Discard any remaining fat. Stir in ¼ cup all-purpose *flour*. Cook and stir over medium heat till bubbly. Remove from the heat. Add enough water or chicken broth to the drippings to equal 2 cups total. Add liquid all at once to flour mixture in pan. Cook and stir till bubbly. Cook and stir 1 minute more. Makes 2 cups.

# Dinner from The Freezer

You needn't settle for anything less than a home-cooked meal—even when there's no time to don your cooking apron.

That's because once you've prepared this make-and-freeze-ahead meal, dinner is at your fingertips. Whether you're looking for one serving or four, just pull the dishes from the freezer; in less than 45 minutes, dinner is served.

## Menu

- Pork and Vegetable Dinner*
- Very Berry Salad*
- Broccoli
- Orange Soufflé*
- Milk

*see pages 80–83*

*Pork and Vegetable Dinner*

# Pork and Vegetable Dinner

¾ **pound boneless pork shoulder**
1 **tablespoon cooking oil**
¾ **cup water**
¼ **cup dry sherry**
2 **tablespoons soy sauce**
¼ **teaspoon ground ginger**
1 **green pepper**
1 **large onion**
1 **cup sliced carrots**
¼ **cup cold water**
4 **teaspoons cornstarch**
**Hot cooked noodles (optional)**

Cut pork into ½-inch cubes (see photo 1). In a skillet brown pork cubes in hot oil. Add ¾ cup water, sherry, soy sauce, and ginger. Cover and simmer for 15 minutes. Meanwhile, cut green pepper into strips and onion into thin wedges (see photo 2). Add green pepper, onion, and carrots. Simmer 15 minutes more or till meat is tender and vegetables are crisp-tender. In a small bowl combine ¼ cup water and cornstarch; stir into meat mixture. Cook and stir till thickened and bubbly, then cook and stir for 2 minutes more. Cool mixture quickly over ice water. Divide mixture among 4 freezer containers, then seal, label, and freeze (see photo 3).

Before serving: Place desired number of portions of frozen pork mixture in a saucepan. Add 1 tablespoon *water* for each portion. Cook, covered, over medium-low heat for 10 to 30 minutes or till heated through, stirring occasionally with a fork (see photo 4). Serve over hot cooked noodles, if desired. Makes 4 servings.

**Microwave directions:** Place 1 frozen portion in a nonmetal dish. Cover with vented clear plastic wrap or waxed paper. In a countertop microwave oven, micro-cook on 100% power (HIGH) for 4 to 5 minutes or till heated through, giving dish a quarter-turn and stirring after 2 minutes. (For 2 servings, cook for 7 to 9 minutes, rearranging twice and stirring after 5 minutes. For 4 servings, cook for 12 to 14 minutes, rearranging twice and stirring after 8 minutes.) Serve over hot cooked noodles, if desired.

**1** Using a sharp knife, cut the pork into ½-inch strips, then into ½-inch cubes. Cutting the pork into uniformly sized pieces helps the meat cook and thaw at an even rate.

**2** Remove the top and seeds from the green pepper; cut it in half lengthwise. Cut the halves lengthwise into strips. Peel the onion. Cut it in half lengthwise, then cut the halves into thin wedges.

**3** Evenly divide the cooled mixture among four individual freezer containers, as shown. Choose containers that are a bit larger than the mixture requires, because the frozen mixture will expand slightly.

Seal the containers and label each of them with the name of the recipe and the date it was prepared. Freeze.

**4** Use a fork to gently break apart the frozen mixture as it thaws. Breaking up the meat and vegetable mixture with a fork speeds up the thawing time and allows more-even heating of the mixture.

# Timetable

**2** days before
- Cook Pork and Vegetable Dinner. Divide the mixture among containers; seal, label, and freeze.
- Prepare Very Berry Salad. Use a blender or food processor to blend the strawberries. After the salads are frozen, transfer them to a moisture- and vaporproof freezer bag, as shown. Freeze.
- Make Orange Soufflés. Cover and freeze.

**40** mins. before
- Preheat the oven to 325°. Remove the desired number of soufflés from the freezer; remove the foil. Place them in a shallow baking pan and pour boiling water around the dishes to a level of ½ inch. Bake about 55 minutes. This will allow the soufflés to finish baking while you eat dinner.

**20** mins. before
- Set the table. Remove the desired number of salads from the freezer. Invert the salads onto lettuce-lined salad plates.
- Place the desired number of frozen Pork and Vegetable Dinners in a saucepan. Reheat according to directions.
- Cook the broccoli and noodles.
- At serving time, garnish each salad with a dollop of salad dressing or mayonnaise, if desired. Pour milk into glasses. Spoon Pork and Vegetable Dinner over hot noodles, if desired. Serve broccoli.
- Just before serving, test the soufflés for doneness. Serve immediately.

# Very Berry Salad

*If you don't have a blender or a food processor, use your mixer to blend the berries. The mixture will have tiny pieces of strawberries in it, but will taste every bit as delicious as the blender version. (Pictured on page 78.)*

¾  **cup sliced strawberries**
1  **8-ounce carton raspberry yogurt**
1  **tablespoon sugar**
   **Lettuce leaves**

Place strawberries in a blender container or food processor bowl. Cover; blend or process till smooth. In a small bowl stir together strawberries, yogurt, and sugar.

Line four 6-ounce custard cups or a muffin pan with paper bake cups, if desired. Evenly divide mixture among the custard cups. Cover; freeze till firm.

Remove salads from custard cups or muffin pan. Place in a moisture- and vaporproof freezer bag. Seal, label, and freeze.

Before serving: Remove desired number of salads from freezer bag. Line each salad plate with lettuce. Remove paper bake cups, if used. Invert frozen salad on top of lettuce-lined plate. Let stand at room temperature for 20 minutes. Dollop with salad dressing or mayonnaise, if desired. Makes 4 servings.

# Attention, Microwave Owners!

Recipes with microwave directions were tested in countertop microwave ovens that operate on 600 to 700 watts. Times are approximates, because microwave ovens vary by manufacturer.

# Orange Soufflés

*Serve these delicate desserts immediately after removing them from the oven.*

2  **tablespoons margarine *or* butter**
3  **tablespoons all-purpose flour**
⅓  **cup milk**
½  **teaspoon finely shredded orange peel**
⅓  **cup orange juice**
2  **egg yolks**
2  **egg whites**
2  **tablespoons sugar**

In a saucepan melt margarine; stir in flour. Add milk. Cook and stir till mixture is very thick and forms a ball. Remove from the heat. Gradually stir in orange peel and juice. In a small mixer bowl beat egg yolks with an electric mixer on high speed for 4 minutes or till thick and lemon colored. Beat on low speed while gradually adding orange mixture. Wash beaters thoroughly.

In a mixer bowl beat egg whites on high speed till soft peaks form (tips curl). Gradually add sugar, beating till stiff peaks form (tips stand straight). Fold orange mixture into egg whites. Evenly divide the soufflé mixture among 4 individual (1-cup) soufflé dishes or 10-ounce custard cups. Cover with foil. Label and freeze.

Before serving: Remove the desired number of soufflés from the freezer; remove foil. Place 1 or 2 frozen soufflés in a shallow 9x9x2-inch baking pan. (If baking 3 or 4 soufflés, use a 12x8x2-inch baking pan.) Pour boiling water into the pan around soufflés to a depth of ½ inch. Bake in a 325° oven about 55 minutes or till knife inserted near center comes out clean. Serves 4.

# Ham On Sale

Taking advantage of specials is one way to beat rising food costs.

Put this guideline into practice by buying a larger ham for this menu. First, slice, dice, and cube the ham. For future meals, freeze the ham slices and cubes for Spicy Peach-Glazed Ham and Ham-Sprout Kabobs. Then, sample Hearty Ham and Potato Chowder tonight.

## Menu

- Hearty Ham and Potato Chowder*
- Corn muffins
- Lettuce wedge with dressing
- Orange Spice Bars*
- Coffee

*see pages 86–89*

*Hearty Ham and Potato Chowder*

# Hearty Ham and Potato Chowder

*This 2¼-pound boneless ham is easily transformed into three different meals—just cut it into desired portions and freeze (see photos 1–3). It's that simple!*

| | |
|---|---|
| ¾ | **pound fully cooked ham** |
| 1½ | **cups peeled, cubed potatoes** |
| 1 | **cup sliced carrots** |
| 1 | **cup water** |
| 2 | **teaspoons instant chicken bouillon granules** |
| ½ | **teaspoon dried basil, crushed** |
| ¾ | **cup sliced celery** |
| 2 | **cups milk** |
| 4 | **teaspoons cornstarch** |
| ⅓ | **cup sliced green onion** |
| ¼ | **cup snipped parsley** |

Dice ham (see photo 4). Set aside. In a large saucepan combine potatoes, carrots, water, bouillon granules, and basil. Bring to boiling; reduce the heat. Cover and simmer for 10 minutes. Add celery; cover and simmer for 5 minutes more or till vegetables are tender.

Stir together milk and cornstarch. Add ham, milk mixture, green onion, and parsley to the saucepan. Cook and stir till thickened and bubbly (see photo 5). Cook and stir for 2 minutes more. Ladle soup into serving bowls. Serves 4.

**1** Starting from the large end of the ham, slice the ham vertically into four ⅜-inch slices. It's important to cut these slices first so they're approximately the same size.

**2** Divide the remaining ham into two equal portions. Set the hind portion aside for the Hearty Ham and Potato Chowder. Cut the remaining ham into 1-inch cubes, as shown.

**3** Store the ham slices and ham cubes for use in future meals. Place the ham slices and ham cubes in separate moisture- and vaporproof freezer bags. Seal, label, and freeze.

**4** To dice ham, cut hind portion into strips, then place the strips together and cut them crosswise into small cubes, as shown. Dicing usually refers to cutting food into pieces about ¼ inch on each side.

**5** Stirring constantly, cook the chowder over medium-high heat till thickened and bubbly. At this stage the mixture will become slightly thick and bubbles should break gently over the entire surface of the chowder.

# Timetable

**1** day before
- Make Orange Spice Bars; bake and allow to cool. Make Orange Icing and frost the bars. Cover.
- Prepare the corn muffins. When they're cool, cover and store them till serving time.

**45** mins. before
- Divide the ham into three portions. Cut up two portions, and dice the remaining ham for Hearty Ham and Potato Chowder. Prepare the chowder.
- Core and thoroughly wash a small head of lettuce; drain. Cut it into wedges. Place each wedge on a salad plate.

## Just Before Serving
- Warm the corn muffins, then place them in a napkin-lined basket or on a plate. Drizzle your favorite salad dressing over the lettuce wedges. Pour coffee into mugs.
- Cut Orange Spice Bars into bars; arrange on a serving plate.

# Orange Spice Bars

*Moist and crumbly, these cakelike bars taste delicious with an ice-cold glass of milk. (Pictured on page 85.)*

½ **cup quick-cooking rolled oats**
½ **cup chopped walnuts**
½ **of a 6-ounce can (⅓ cup) frozen orange juice concentrate, thawed**
⅓ **cup water**
¼ **cup raisins**
1¾ **cups all-purpose flour**
1 **teaspoon baking soda**
1 **teaspoon ground ginger**
1 **teaspoon ground cinnamon**
¼ **teaspoon salt**
½ **cup margarine *or* butter**
½ **cup sugar**
½ **cup molasses**
1 **egg**
**Orange Icing**

In a medium bowl stir together oats, walnuts, orange juice concentrate, water, and raisins; set aside. In a separate bowl stir together flour, soda, ginger, cinnamon, and salt; set aside.

In a mixer bowl beat margarine or butter and sugar with an electric mixer till light and fluffy. Beat in molasses and egg. (Mixture will appear curdled.) Add raisin and flour mixtures alternately to beaten mixture, beating well after each addition. Turn into a greased 13x9x2-inch baking pan. Bake in a 325° oven for 30 to 35 minutes or till done. Cool completely. Frost with Orange Icing. Makes 36 bars.

**Orange Icing:** In a small mixing bowl stir together 1½ cups sifted *powdered sugar* and 4 to 6 teaspoons *orange juice.*

# Spicy Peach-Glazed Ham

*Brush ham slices with additional peach preserves just before serving to give them an extra-peachy flavor.*

¾ **pound fully cooked ham, cut into ⅜-inch-thick slices**
3 **tablespoons peach preserves**
⅛ **teaspoon ground cinnamon**
⅛ **teaspoon ground cloves**

Arrange frozen ham slices in an 11x7x1½-inch baking pan, overlapping if necessary. In a mixing bowl stir together preserves, cinnamon, and cloves. Spread ham slices with preserve mixture. Bake, covered, in a 350° oven about 45 minutes or till ham is heated through. Serves 4.

# Ham-Sprout Kabobs

1 **10-ounce package frozen brussels sprouts**
16 **new potatoes *or* 4 medium potatoes, quartered**
⅓ **cup dry white wine *or* apple juice**
2 **tablespoons lemon juice**
1 **tablespoon cooking oil**
½ **teaspoon dried dillweed**
¾ **pound fully cooked ham, cut into 1-inch cubes**

Cook brussels sprouts according to package directions; drain. Meanwhile, scrub potatoes. Peel a strip around the center of each new potato. Cook, covered, in boiling salted water for 10 to 15 minutes or till tender. Drain and cool.

In a plastic bag combine wine or apple juice, lemon juice, oil, and dillweed. Add brussels sprouts, potatoes, and ham. Close bag tightly. Marinate in the refrigerator overnight, turning occasionally. Drain, reserving marinade. Using eight 8- or 9-inch skewers, alternately thread sprouts, potatoes, and ham. Place kabobs on an unheated rack in a broiler pan. Broil 4 inches from the heat for 10 minutes, turning twice. Brush with reserved marinade often. Serves 4.

# Versatile Chicken

From two chickens you get three delicious meals! How? Buy two whole chickens and cut them up yourself to save extra cents. Try delicate Orange-Sauced Chicken with the menu below, then freeze the remaining chicken pieces and use them later in Chicken and Dumpling Stew and Herbed Chicken and Vegetables.

## Menu

- Orange-Sauced Chicken*

- Buttered peas

- Hard rolls

- Chocolate-Filled Meringues*

- Iced tea

*see pages 92-95*

*Orange-Sauced Chicken*

# Orange-Sauced Chicken

*Cut two chickens into pieces (see photos 1–4), then use both chicken breasts in this delicious dish.*

2 **whole medium chicken breasts (about 1½ pounds total), skinned and halved lengthwise**
¾ **cup orange juice**
1 **tablespoon brown sugar**
1 **tablespoon vinegar**
½ **teaspoon instant chicken bouillon granules**
1 **orange**
2 **tablespoons cold water**
1 **tablespoon cornstarch**
**Leaf lettuce**

Place chicken breast halves meaty side down in an 8x8x2-inch baking dish. In a small bowl stir together orange juice, brown sugar, vinegar, and bouillon granules; pour over chicken. Bake in a 350° oven for 35 to 40 minutes or till chicken is tender.

Meanwhile, cut peel from orange. Discard half of the peel. Remove the white membrane from the remaining half of the peel (see photo 5). Cut the peel into julienne strips (see photo 6). Cook strips of peel, covered, in a small amount of boiling water for 15 minutes. Drain. Section orange and set aside.

Remove chicken, reserving juices. Cover chicken with foil and keep warm. Transfer reserved juices to a small saucepan. Stir together the cold water and cornstarch; add to saucepan. Cook and stir till thickened and bubbly, then cook and stir for 2 minutes more. Add orange sections and peel; heat through. To serve, line a serving platter with lettuce leaves. Arrange chicken on lettuce. Pour sauce over chicken. Serves 4.

**1** Pull the drumstick away from the body. Using a sharp knife, cut through the skin between the thigh and the body. Bend the thigh back until the thighbone pops out of the hip joint. Cut through the broken joint to separate.

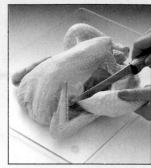

**2** Hold the wing tip and pull it away from the body. Using a sharp knife, slit the skin between the wing and body. Bend the wing back until the wing-body joint breaks. Separate by cutting through the broken joint.

**3** Next, separate the thigh from the leg by slitting the skin above the knee joint. Break the joint by bending the leg and thigh together. Cut through the broken joint, as shown. Repeat with the other leg-thigh piece.

**4** Separate the breast from the back by cutting along the breast end of the ribs on each side, as shown. Pull the front and back halves apart, exposing the joints at the neck, which connect the two halves. Cut through the joints.

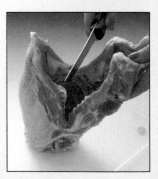

**5** Using a spoon, scoop the bitter, white membrane from the orange peel, as shown. Continue scraping the peel until as much of the membrane as possible is removed.

**6** Using a sharp knife, cut the orange peel into long, thin strips, as shown. The peel adds both flavor and color to the delicate sauce.

# Timetable

| | | |
|---|---|---|
| **3** hrs. before | • Rinse and pat both of the chickens dry. Cut them into pieces. Set the breasts aside, then wrap and freeze the remaining chicken pieces.<br>• Make the meringues, as shown. Prepare the pudding and place it in the refrigerator to chill. For ease, you can prepare the meringues and the pudding the night before. |  |
| **45** mins. before | • Set the oven to 350°. Skin and halve the chicken breasts. Prepare the orange juice mixture and place the chicken in the oven to begin baking.<br>• Meanwhile, cut orange peel from the orange and remove the bitter white membrane, as shown. Cut the orange peel into thin strips, then section the orange. Set the table. |  |
| **Just Before Serving** | • Heat the peas. Warm the rolls, if desired.<br>• Remove the chicken from the baking pan, reserving the juices. Prepare the sauce for the chicken.<br>• Pour iced tea into ice-filled glasses.<br>• Fill the meringues with chilled pudding. Garnish with maraschino cherries. |  |

# Chocolate-Filled Meringues

*Have these meringue shells ready whenever you are. Just place the cooled shells in a moisture- and vapor-proof bag and freeze.*

**2  egg whites**
**½  teaspoon vanilla**
**¼  teaspoon cream of tartar**
**½  cup sugar**
**⅔  cup sugar**
**4  teaspoons cornstarch**
**1½  cups milk**
**1½  squares (1½ ounces) unsweetened chocolate, chopped**
**2  beaten egg yolks**
**2  tablespoons margarine *or* butter**
**1  teaspoon vanilla**
**4  maraschino cherries**

Let egg whites come to room temperature. Meanwhile, line a baking sheet with plain brown paper. Draw four 4-inch circles on the paper. In a small mixer bowl combine egg whites, ½ teaspoon vanilla, and cream of tartar. Beat with an electric mixer on medium speed till soft peaks form (tips curl). Gradually add ½ cup sugar, beating on high speed till stiff peaks form (tips stand straight) and sugar is almost dissolved.

Place a mound of meringue on each circle. Using the back of a spoon, shape meringue into shells. Bake in a 300° oven for 35 minutes. (For crisper meringues, turn off oven. Dry shells in oven with the door closed for 1 hour more.)

Meanwhile, in a heavy saucepan stir together ⅔ cup sugar, cornstarch, and ¼ teaspoon *salt*. Stir in milk and chocolate. Cook and stir over medium heat till thickened and bubbly, then cook and stir for 2 minutes more. Remove from the heat. Gradually stir about *1 cup* hot mixture into egg yolks. Return to saucepan. Cook and stir for 2 minutes more. Remove from the heat. Stir in margarine or butter and 1 teaspoon vanilla. Pour into a bowl. Cover surface of the pudding with clear plastic wrap. Chill without stirring. Before serving, spoon pudding into meringue shells. Top each with a cherry. Serves 4.

# Chocolate Cheesecakes

*For a different dessert, substitute these exquisite miniature cheesecakes for Chocolate-Filled Meringues.*

**Margarine *or* butter**
**¼  cup finely crushed graham crackers *or* finely crushed vanilla wafers (8 to 10)**
**1  tablespoon margarine *or* butter, melted**
**1  3-ounce package cream cheese, softened**
**½  teaspoon vanilla**
**¼  cup sugar**
**1  tablespoon unsweetened cocoa powder**
**1  egg**
**1  tablespoon milk**
**Orange slices, strawberry halves, *or* pineapple chunks (optional)**

Butter the sides and bottoms of 4 muffin cups. In a bowl combine graham crackers or vanilla wafers and margarine or butter; toss. Divide mixture evenly among muffin cups. Press onto bottoms of cups to form a firm crust.

In a small mixer bowl beat cream cheese and vanilla with an electric mixer till fluffy. Gradually add sugar and cocoa powder; beat till combined. Add egg and milk, beating on low speed just till combined. *Do not* overbeat. Pour into muffin cups. Bake in a 350° oven for 15 to 20 minutes or till the center appears set. Cool.

Chill for 2 hours or till serving time. Loosen sides of cheesecakes with a narrow spatula; remove from muffin cups. Place each cheesecake on an individual serving plate. If desired, garnish with an orange slice, strawberry half, or pineapple chunk. Makes 4 servings.

# Chicken and Dumpling Stew

1 **cup assorted vegetable peelings (carrot, potato, turnip, parsnip, *or* other peelings)**
4 **chicken thighs**
2 **chicken backs**
1 **bay leaf**
1 **16-ounce can tomatoes, cut up**
2 **cups canned *or* frozen corn, peas, green beans, and/*or* wax beans**
½ **cup chopped onion**
½ **teaspoon poultry seasoning *or* ground sage**
½ **teaspoon dried basil, crushed**
¼ **cup all-purpose flour**
1 **cup all-purpose flour**
1½ **teaspoons baking powder**
½ **cup milk**
2 **tablespoons cooking oil**
½ **cup shredded American cheese (2 ounces)**

In a 3-quart saucepan combine vegetable peelings, chicken, bay leaf, 3 cups *water,* ¾ teaspoon *salt,* and ¼ teaspoon *pepper.* Bring to boiling; reduce the heat. Cover and simmer for 1 hour. Remove chicken. Strain broth. When chicken is cool enough to handle, remove and discard skin and bones. Cut up chicken. Skim fat from broth. Reserve 2 cups broth; *freeze remainder for another use.*

In the same saucepan combine reserved 2 cups broth and chicken. Stir in *undrained* tomatoes, vegetables, onion, poultry seasoning or sage, and basil. Bring to boiling; reduce the heat. Cover and simmer for 5 minutes. Stir together ½ cup cold *water* and ¼ cup flour. Stir into chicken mixture. Cook and stir till thickened and bubbly, then cook and stir for 1 minute more. To make dumplings, in a bowl stir together 1 cup flour, baking powder, and ¼ teaspoon *salt.* Stir together milk and cooking oil. Add to dry ingredients, stirring just till moistened. Drop dough from tablespoon to make 6 to 8 mounds

atop bubbling stew. Cover tightly and simmer for 15 minutes or till a wooden toothpick inserted in a dumpling comes out clean. Sprinkle dumplings with cheese. Makes 4 servings.

# Herbed Chicken and Vegetables

4 **chicken drumsticks**
4 **chicken wings**
1 **tablespoon cooking oil**
½ **cup water**
½ **cup dry white wine**
1 **clove garlic, minced**
1 **teaspoon instant chicken bouillon granules**
1 **teaspoon dried thyme, crushed**
1 **16-ounce package loose-pack frozen mixed broccoli, carrots, and onions**
4 **ounces medium noodles**
2 **tablespoons cold water**
1 **tablespoon cornstarch**

In a medium skillet brown chicken in hot oil for 10 to 15 minutes, turning to brown evenly. Remove from the heat. Drain off fat. Season chicken with salt and pepper. Add ½ cup water, wine, garlic, bouillon granules, and thyme. Bring to boiling; reduce the heat. Cover and simmer for 30 minutes. Add vegetables; simmer for 5 to 10 minutes more or till chicken is tender.

Meanwhile, cook noodles according to package directions. Drain. Place noodles on a serving platter. Arrange chicken on top. Cover with foil to keep warm. Skim fat from pan juices.

Stir together 2 tablespoons cold water and cornstarch; add to skillet. Cook and stir till thickened and bubbly, then cook and stir for 2 minutes more. Spoon vegetable mixture over chicken and noodles. Makes 4 servings.

◄ *Pictured opposite: Herbed Chicken and Vegetables*

# Country Brunch

If you're thinking about entertaining a small crowd, why not brunch it? A cross between breakfast and lunch, this hearty meal will satisfy your guests—and your pocketbook.

## Menu

- Eggs and Sausage Scramble*
- Buttermilk Crepes*
- Pineapple-Cheese Topping*
- Cranberry Syrup*
- Tropical Fruit Fandango*
- Coffee

*see pages 100-103

*Buttermilk Crepes*

# Buttermilk Crepes

*Keep crepes on hand for unexpected occasions. Make crepes as directed, then wrap them individually in clear plastic wrap. Place the crepes in a freezer container and freeze them for up to 2 months. Or, place the folded crepes in a covered container and chill thoroughly.*

3  **eggs**
1¼  **cups buttermilk**
1  **cup all-purpose flour**
¾  **cup milk**
4  **teaspoons cooking oil**
2  **teaspoons sugar**
⅛  **teaspoon salt**
½  **cup margarine *or* butter, softened**

In a bowl combine eggs, buttermilk, flour, milk, oil, sugar, and salt. Beat with a rotary beater (see photo 1). Heat a lightly greased 6-inch skillet over high heat. Remove from the heat. Spoon in about *2 tablespoons* of batter (see photo 2). Lift and tilt skillet to spread batter. Return to the heat; brown 1 side only. Invert pan over paper towel to remove crepe. Repeat to make about 24 crepes, greasing skillet occasionally.

Spread about *1 teaspoon* margarine on unbrowned side of each crepe (see photo 3). Fold crepes in half, browned side out; fold in half again to form a triangle (see photo 4). Place folded crepes on a serving platter. Keep warm. Makes 24.

**To reheat conventionally:** Place the frozen crepes in a 15x10x1-inch baking pan. Cover with foil. Bake crepes in a 350° oven about 20 minutes. Or, if crepes are chilled, bake in a 350° oven for 10 to 15 minutes.

**To reheat in microwave:** Place 12 frozen crepes on a nonmetal plate lined with paper towels. Cover with another paper towel. In a countertop microwave cook, on 100% power (HIGH), for 3 to 4 minutes or till heated through, rearranging crepes and giving dish a half-turn after 2 minutes. Repeat with the remaining crepes.

**1** Using a rotary beater, beat the ingredients till the batter is smooth and has no lumps. If you don't have a rotary beater, you can use a wire whisk or an electric mixer.

**2** Pour about 2 tablespoons of the batter into a heated skillet. Immediately lift and tilt the skillet, rotating it so that the batter covers the bottom of the skillet in an even layer.

**3** Use a small spatula or a knife to spread about 1 teaspoon margarine on the unbrowned side of each crepe. This thin layer of margarine prevents the crepes from becoming gummy.

**4** Fold each crepe in half, browned side out. Fold it in half again to form a triangle. Folding the crepes makes them easier to serve and eat. The browned outside makes them more attractive, too.

# Timetable

| | | |
|---|---|---|
| **1** day before | • Prepare Tropical Fruit Fandango; cover and chill.<br>• Next, prepare Buttermilk Crepes. Cover and chill. Place the folded crepes in a 15x10x1-inch pan. Or, make up the crepes several days or weeks ahead and freeze them. Then, reheat the crepes just before serving. |  |
| **1½** hrs. before | • If you don't have anyone helping you, set the table now. This will give you some extra time later, when you're making last-minute preparations.<br>• Prepare the crepe toppings. |  |
| **35** mins. before | • Prepare Eggs and Sausage Scramble. Lift and fold the mixture to cook the eggs and scramble the mixture.<br>• Reheat the frozen or chilled crepes in a conventional oven. If you plan to use a microwave oven, reheat the crepes about 10 minutes before serving. |  |
| **At Serving Time** | • Divide the Tropical Fruit Fandango into 12 individual serving dishes.<br>• Place the crepe toppings in small serving bowls or small serving pitchers.<br>• Pour freshly brewed coffee into mugs. |  |

# Eggs and Sausage Scramble

*Snazzy scrambled eggs! (Pictured on page 98.)*

16 **eggs**
1 **cup milk**
1 **8-ounce package brown-and-serve**
 **sausage links, cut into ½-inch pieces**
1 **tablespoon cooking oil**
3 **medium potatoes, peeled and chopped**
½ **cup chopped green pepper**
2 **tablespoons margarine *or* butter**

In a bowl beat together eggs, milk, ¼ teaspoon *salt*, and ¼ teaspoon *pepper*; set aside. In a 10-inch skillet cook sausage in hot oil about 4 minutes or till brown. Add potatoes; cook and stir for 3 minutes. Add green pepper; cook and stir about 2 minutes more or till vegetables are crisp-tender. Keep warm.

In a 12-inch skillet melt margarine or butter over medium heat. Add egg mixture. Cook over medium heat, without stirring, about 5 minutes or till mixture begins to set on the bottom and around the edges. Spoon sausage and vegetables over egg mixture. Using a spatula, lift and fold partially cooked eggs so uncooked portion flows underneath and sausage and vegetables are mixed into egg mixture. Continue cooking over medium heat for 3 to 4 minutes or till eggs are cooked throughout but are still glossy and moist. Makes 12 servings.

# Pineapple-Cheese Topping

1 **3-ounce package cream cheese,**
 **softened**
¼ **cup pineapple *or* strawberry topping**
2 **tablespoons milk**

In a small mixer bowl beat cream cheese with an electric mixer till smooth. Add topping and milk; beat till smooth. If desired, cook over low heat till heated through. Makes ⅔ cup.

# Tropical Fruit Fandango

*It's a combination of juicy pineapple chunks, tangy oranges and apples, and island-grown coconut that gives this salad an unforgettable fruity flavor. (Pictured on page 98.)*

1 **20-ounce can pineapple chunks**
 **(juice pack)**
1 **tablespoon cornstarch**
¼ **teaspoon ground ginger**
3 **medium tart apples, cored and sliced**
 **into thin wedges**
3 **small oranges, peeled and sectioned**
¼ **cup coconut, toasted**

Drain pineapple, reserving ¾ *cup* juice. For dressing, in a small saucepan combine reserved juice, cornstarch, and ginger. Cook and stir till thickened and bubbly, then cook and stir for 2 minutes more. Set aside to cool slightly.

In a mixing bowl combine pineapple, apples, and oranges; toss. Pour dressing over fruit; toss. Chill for at least 3 hours. Evenly divide fruit mixture among 12 serving dishes. Sprinkle with toasted coconut. Makes 12 servings.

# Cranberry Syrup

*A delicious, sweet-tart syrup with a hint of cinnamon. (Pictured on page 99.)*

2 **tablespoons margarine *or* butter**
1 **tablespoon cornstarch**
¾ **cup cranberry juice cocktail**
¼ **cup packed brown sugar**
⅛ **teaspoon ground cinnamon**

In a small saucepan melt margarine or butter; stir in cornstarch. Stir in cranberry juice cocktail, sugar, and cinnamon. Cook and stir till thickened and bubbly, then cook and stir for 2 minutes more. Makes about ¾ cup syrup.

# Participation Dinner

Share expenses and cooking chores by letting your guests participate in your next dinner party.

Give your guests their recipes about two weeks before the party so they'll have plenty of time to plan their strategy. Assign Seafood Dip to one couple, Cool Cucumber Salad to a second couple, and Luscious Lemon Torte to a third couple.

## Menu

- Wine Spritzers*
- Seafood Dip*
- Nutty Rice-Stuffed Chicken*
- Cool Cucumber Salad*
- Luscious Lemon Torte*

*see pages 106–109

*Nutty Rice-Stuffed Chicken*

# Nutty Rice-Stuffed Chicken

1⅓ cups water
⅔ cup Savory Rice Mix (see recipe, page 26)
¾ teaspoon dried basil, crushed
½ cup chopped pecans
4 whole medium chicken breasts (3 pounds total), halved lengthwise
1½ cups milk
2 tablespoons cornstarch
½ cup shredded American cheese (2 ounces)
1 4-ounce can mushroom stems and pieces, drained
1 teaspoon dried parsley flakes
3 10-ounce packages frozen chopped spinach

In a small saucepan combine water, Savory Rice Mix, and basil. Bring to boiling. Reduce the heat, then simmer, covered, for 15 minutes. Do not lift the cover. Remove from the heat. Stir in pecans. Let stand, covered, for 10 minutes. Fluff with a fork (see photo 1). Set aside.

Using a sharp knife, cut a pocket in each chicken breast half (see photo 2). Sprinkle pockets with salt and pepper. Spoon about ¼ cup stuffing into each pocket (see photo 3). Arrange chicken in a 15x10x1-inch baking pan (see photo 4). Bake in a 350° oven for 35 to 40 minutes or till tender.

Meanwhile, in a saucepan stir together milk and cornstarch. Cook and stir till thickened and bubbly, then cook and stir for 2 minutes more. Stir in cheese till melted (see photo 5). Add mushrooms and parsley. Heat through. Cook spinach according to package directions. Drain thoroughly. Transfer spinach to a large serving platter. Arrange chicken on top. Serve mushroom sauce with chicken. Makes 8 servings.

**1** After the rice is done cooking, let it stand for 10 minutes to absorb any remaining liquid. Then, fluff the rice with a fork, as shown, to separate the rice grains.

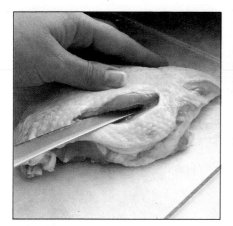

**2** Insert a sharp knife between the meat and rib bones. Cut a pocket parallel to the bones, 3 to 4 inches long and 2 inches deep. Repeat with remaining chicken breasts.

**3** Using a tablespoon, carefully spoon about ¼ cup of the stuffing into each pocket. The pockets should be full and it may be necessary to mound some of the stuffing.

**4** Carefully arrange the stuffed chicken breast halves in the baking pan, making sure the stuffing does not fall out. Space them as evenly as possible.

**5** After the milk-cornstarch mixture thickens, add the cheese. Stir till the cheese is completely melted. Using a process cheese, like American, gives the sauce a smooth, creamy appearance. Never use a natural cheese, like cheddar; natural cheeses give sauces a grainy, curdled appearance.

# Timetable

**1** day before
● Add sparkle to your Wine Spritzers by using fruited ice cubes. Prepare the fruited cubes, as shown. Freeze. Chill both the wine and the carbonated beverage.

**1½** hrs. before
● Cook the Savory Rice Mix. Stuff the chicken breast halves, then bake. Prepare the mushroom sauce that accompanies the chicken. Cover with plastic wrap. Set aside.

**30** mins. before
● As guests arrive with the appetizer, salad, and dessert, chill the salad and dessert. Serve the appetizer.
● Combine the chilled wine and carbonated beverage; mix gently. Pour over the fruited ice cubes in glasses. Serve with the appetizer.

**10** mins. before
● Cook the spinach. Meanwhile, reheat the mushroom sauce. Place the spinach on a serving platter. Next, carefully arrange the chicken on top of the spinach. Place the salad on the table.
● Just before serving the dessert, cut the torte into slices, as shown.

# Seafood Dip

*The inexpensive seafood product used in this dip is made from fish, but you'll be surprised by how much it tastes like crabmeat!*

1   8-ounce carton dairy sour cream
½   cup salad dressing *or* mayonnaise
1   tablespoon snipped parsley
1   teaspoon lemon juice
1   teaspoon Worcestershire sauce
½   teaspoon grated onion
1   6-ounce package frozen imitation crab
      fingers, thawed (1⅓ cups)
      Assorted crackers and vegetables*

In a small bowl stir together sour cream, salad dressing or mayonnaise, parsley, lemon juice, Worcestershire sauce, and onion. Cut or flake crab fingers into small pieces. Stir into sour cream mixture. Chill. Serve dip with an assortment of crackers and vegetables. Makes 2 cups.

**Note:** Choose from celery sticks, cherry tomatoes, sweet potato slices, green onions, green pepper cubes or strips, cauliflower flowerets, sliced summer squash, or broccoli flowerets.

# Cool Cucumber Salad

3   small cucumbers
2   medium tomatoes
¾   cup vinegar
½   cup sugar
3   tablespoons salad oil
¾   teaspoon dried thyme, crushed
4   cups torn salad greens

Score cucumbers by running a fork lengthwise down each cucumber. Cut into thin slices. Core and chop tomatoes. In a bowl combine cucumbers and tomatoes. In a screw-top jar combine vinegar, sugar, oil, thyme, dash *salt,* and dash *pepper.* Cover and shake well. Pour over vegetables; stir gently. Cover. Chill for 2 to 24 hours, stirring occasionally. Before serving, drain vegetables. Add greens and toss. Serves 8.

# Luscious Lemon Torte

¾   cup sugar
2   tablespoons cornstarch
⅛   teaspoon ground ginger
¾   cup water
1   slightly beaten egg yolk
1   teaspoon finely shredded lemon peel
3   tablespoons lemon juice
1   tablespoon margarine *or* butter
1   10¾-ounce frozen loaf pound cake,
      thawed
1   4-ounce container frozen whipped
      dessert topping, thawed

For filling, in a small saucepan stir together sugar, cornstarch, ginger, and dash *salt.* Add water and egg yolk. Cook and stir over medium-high heat till thickened and bubbly, then cook and stir for 2 minutes more. Remove from the heat. Stir in lemon peel, lemon juice, and margarine or butter. Chill in an ice bath for 5 minutes.

Meanwhile, split pound cake horizontally into 4 layers. To assemble torte, spread about ⅓ cup filling between layers. Frost top and sides with dessert topping. Chill for several hours or overnight. Garnish with lemon slices or shredded lemon peel, if desired. Slice torte. Serves 8.

# Wine Spritzers

1   26½-ounce bottle (3⅓ cups) dry white *or*
      rosé wine, chilled
1   16-ounce bottle (2 cups) carbonated
      lemon-lime beverage *or* carbonated
      water
      Fruited ice cubes* *or* ice cubes

Pour wine into a large pitcher. Add carbonated beverage or carbonated water. Gently stir. Fill 8 wineglasses with fruited ice cubes. Pour about ⅔ cup wine mixture into each glass. Serves 8.

**Note:** For fruited ice cubes, fill ice cube trays with water. Place 1 *strawberry, orange twist,* or *lemon twist* in each compartment of tray; freeze.

# Company Dinner For Four

Your guests will never suspect this showy meal was tailored to a budget. Round steak transformed into tender Stuffed Steak Rolls is the main event in this dazzling dinner. Supporting stars include nutty Peanut Pilaf, garden-fresh Spinach-Iceberg Salad, and for the grand finale, ice-cream-filled Individual Alaskas.

## Menu

- Stuffed Steak Rolls*
- Buttered carrots
- Peanut Pilaf*
- Spinach-Iceberg Salad*
- Individual Alaskas*

*see pages 112–115

*Stuffed Steak Rolls*

# Stuffed Steak Rolls

1 **pound beef top round steak,
   cut ½ inch thick**
½ **of a 10-ounce package (1 cup) frozen
   chopped broccoli, thawed and drained**
1 **tablespoon grated Parmesan cheese**
1 **clove garlic, minced**
¼ **teaspoon dried basil, crushed**
1 **tablespoon cooking oil**
⅓ **cup water**
2 **tablespoons dry white wine**
½ **teaspoon instant beef bouillon granules**
½ **teaspoon Worcestershire sauce**
1 **tablespoon cold water**
2 **teaspoons cornstarch**
   **Peanut Pilaf *or* hot cooked rice**
   **Parsley sprigs (optional)**
   **Radishes (optional)**

Cut meat into 4 serving-size pieces. Pound each piece with the coarse-toothed side of a meat mallet till meat is about ¼ inch thick. In a small bowl stir together broccoli, Parmesan cheese, garlic, and basil. Spoon about *¼ cup* broccoli mixture on *each* piece of meat. Roll up jelly-roll style, starting from short side; tie with string or fasten with wooden toothpicks (see photo 1). In a skillet brown meat rolls in hot oil slowly on all sides (see photo 2). Transfer meat rolls to an 8x8x2-inch baking dish or pan. Stir together ⅓ cup water, wine, bouillon granules, and Worcestershire sauce; pour over meat. Cover and bake in a 350° oven for 30 minutes. Uncover; bake about 10 minutes more or till tender.

To make sauce, measure cooking liquid. If necessary, add enough water to measure ¾ cup. In a small saucepan stir together 1 tablespoon cold water and cornstarch. Stir in ¾ cup cooking liquid (see photo 3). Cook and stir till thickened and bubbly, then cook and stir for 2 minutes more. Remove string or toothpicks (see photo 4). Arrange steak rolls atop Peanut Pilaf or hot rice. Pour sauce over. Garnish with parsley sprigs and radishes, if desired. Makes 4 servings.

**1** Starting at the short end of the piece of meat, roll up the meat, as shown. Tie both ends with string to secure the meat rolls. Or, insert wooden toothpicks at both ends of the rolls.

**2** Place the meat rolls in the hot oil. Cook, turning frequently with tongs, to thoroughly brown all sides. Browning the meat before it goes into the oven gives the meat a darker, richer color and helps develop a richer flavor.

**3** Pour the cooking liquid into the saucepan, stirring as you pour. The cornstarch mixture should already be in the saucepan. Dissolving the cornstarch in cold water before adding the hot cooking liquid helps prevent the sauce from lumping.

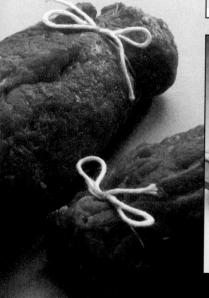

**4** Using the kitchen shears or a knife, cut the string from the meat rolls and discard. If you use toothpicks, carefully pull from the meat rolls and discard.

# Timetable

| | | |
|---|---|---|
| **1¼** hrs. before | • Place scoops of your favorite flavor of ice cream on cookies for Individual Alaskas; freeze.<br>• Start the Stuffed Steak Rolls. Spoon filling on the meat and roll up; secure with string or wooden toothpicks. Brown the meat rolls and transfer them to a baking dish or pan. |  |
| **50** mins. before | • Cover the meat rolls with foil and bake. Uncover the meat during the last 10 minutes to finish browning.<br>• Thoroughly rinse the spinach and iceberg lettuce and drain. Tear the greens into bite-size pieces, as shown. Prepare the salad dressing and chill. |  |
| **40** mins. before | • Start the Peanut Pilaf cooking. Meanwhile, wash and trim 5 or 6 medium carrots. Cut the carrots into julienne strips, as shown. Cook the carrots, covered, in a small amount of boiling salted water for 10 to 15 minutes or till crisp-tender. |  |
| **At Serving Time** | • Remove the meat rolls from the baking pan or dish, reserving the cooking juices. Cover the meat with foil to keep it warm. Make the sauce, as shown. Place Peanut Pilaf on a serving platter. Arrange the meat rolls on top and pour sauce over the meat.<br>• Pour salad dressing over the salad and toss. If you want more crunch in your salad, top it with croutons. |  |
| **Just Before Dessert** | • Turn the oven on to 500°. Prepare the egg white meringue. Remove the baking sheet from the freezer. Spread the ice cream mounds with meringue. Bake in the preheated oven as directed. Serve coffee with dessert, if desired. |  |

# Peanut Pilaf

*Peanut butter makes it delightfully different—hot rice with a peanutty punch. (Pictured on page 110.)*

1⅓   cups water
⅔   cup medium grain rice
2   tablespoons snipped parsley
2   tablespoons margarine *or* butter
2   tablespoons peanut butter
1   teaspoon instant chicken bouillon
       granules
2   tablespoons chopped peanuts

In a small saucepan combine water, rice, parsley, margarine or butter, peanut butter, and bouillon granules. Bring to boiling. Reduce the heat, then simmer, covered, for 15 minutes; do not lift the cover. Remove from the heat. Stir in peanuts. Let stand, covered, for 10 minutes. Fluff rice with a fork. Makes 4 servings.

# Individual Alaskas

4   3-inch chocolate chip, chocolate,
       peanut butter, *or* sugar cookies
1   cup ice cream
2   egg whites
½   teaspoon vanilla
⅛   teaspoon cream of tartar
⅓   cup sugar

Arrange cookies several inches apart on a baking sheet. Place ¼ cup scooped ice cream on each cookie. Place in the freezer.

At serving time, to prepare meringue, in a small mixer bowl beat egg whites, vanilla, and cream of tartar with an electric mixer on high speed till soft peaks form (tips curl). Gradually add sugar, beating till stiff peaks form (tips stand straight). Spread ice cream with meringue, sealing to edge of cookie and baking sheet. Swirl meringue to make decorative peaks. Bake in a 500° oven about 2 minutes or till golden. Serve immediately. Makes 4 servings.

# Spinach-Iceberg Salad

*A simple, scrumptious salad. (Pictured on page 110.)*

2   cups torn spinach
2   cups torn iceberg lettuce
½   cup sliced radishes
1   hard-cooked egg, finely chopped
¼   cup salad dressing *or* mayonnaise
¼   cup dairy sour cream
2   tablespoons thinly sliced green onion
2   tablespoons milk
⅛   teaspoon garlic powder
¼   cup croutons (optional)

In a salad bowl combine spinach, lettuce, radishes, and egg. Toss. Cover and chill.

Meanwhile, make dressing. Stir together salad dressing or mayonnaise, sour cream, onion, milk, and garlic powder. Cover and chill. Before serving, stir additional milk into dressing for desired consistency, if necessary. Pour over salad; toss. Sprinkle with croutons, if desired. Serves 4.

# Homemade Croutons

Save money by making your own croutons. Just prepare croutons, then keep them on hand for fast fix-ups.

Brush bread slices lightly with melted margarine. Cut the bread into ½-inch cubes; sprinkle with garlic powder or your favorite crushed dried herb, if desired. Spread on a baking sheet. Bake in a 300° oven for 20 to 25 minutes or till the croutons are dry and crisp. Cool. Store in a covered container.

# Be Creative With Leftovers

One time-tested way to stretch your food dollar is to use all of the food you buy. To help, here are some hints on how to use every morsel of food. We've also included a recipe that shows you how to create a pot pie from a variety of leftover meats and vegetables.

**Bountiful bread**
● When you have bread that has lost some of its freshness or have the "heels" left over, use them for French toast, strata casseroles, or bread pudding.
● Or, cube bread and toast the cubes for croutons, then toss them into a salad or sprinkle them atop soup or a casserole.
● Crumble dry bread for a topping for casseroles or creamed vegetables. Store the crumbs in the freezer.

**Bits and pieces**
Stash a "collectibles" quart container in your freezer. Add bits of

vegetables, rice, and meat to the container. When you have a quart's worth of goodies, cook meaty soup bones. Then add the goodies and seasonings for a delicious soup.

**Extra eggs**
● Poach egg yolks till firm, then sieve or finely chop them. The yolks add color and flavor to sandwich fillings and make a great garnish.
● Keep leftover raw egg whites, covered, in the refrigerator. Use for angel cakes, frostings, meringues, and puddings. Or, add them to a meat loaf mixture.

# Pick-a-Pot Pie

*Choose any cooked meat and vegetable you like.*

½ **cup chopped celery**
½ **cup chopped onion**
¼ **cup chopped green pepper**
3 **tablespoons margarine *or* butter**
½ **cup all-purpose flour**
¼ **teaspoon dried rosemary *or* thyme, crushed**
1 **cup chicken *or* beef broth**
1 **cup milk**
2 **cups cubed cooked beef, ham, pork, chicken, turkey, *or* two 7-ounce cans tuna, drained**
1 **cup cooked peas, carrots, green beans, corn, *or* mixed vegetables**
**Parmesan Points, Quick Biscuit Topper, *or* Cheesy Dumplings**

In a large saucepan cook celery, onion, and green pepper in hot margarine or butter till tender. Stir in flour, rosemary or thyme, and ⅛ teaspoon *pepper*. Stir in broth and milk all at once. Cook and stir till thickened and bubbly, then cook and stir for 1 minute more. Stir in meat and vegetables. Pour into a 1½-quart casserole. Top with desired topper. Bake in a 425° oven for 15 to 20 minutes or till heated through and dumplings or biscuits are done. Let stand for 5 minutes. Makes 6 servings.

**Parmesan Points:** Cut 3 slices *bread* diagonally into 4 triangles each. Place around edge of casserole, overlapping, if necessary. Drizzle 2 tablespoons melted *margarine or butter* on top of bread slices. Sprinkle with 1 to 2 tablespoons grated *Parmesan cheese*. Bake as directed.

**Quick Biscuit Topper:** Snip 1 package (6) *refrigerated biscuits* into quarters. Place the biscuits on top of mixture. Bake as directed.

**Cheesy Dumplings:** Stir together 1 cup *packaged biscuit mix,* ½ cup shredded *American cheese,* and ¼ cup *milk.* Drop by spoonfuls onto hot mixture. Bake as directed.

# Money-Saving Moxie

The secret to mealtime savings is as simple as A-B-C.

*A* list. Shop with a detailed list of grocery needs.

*Be* organized. Nothing wastes money and time faster than aimlessly wandering supermarket aisles and picking up unnecessary food items.

*C*areful planning. Plan weekly menus. No more wasting money and time in extra trips to the store for an unplanned dinner.

You'll appreciate the super savings you've made when it's time to balance your checkbook.

### Starting out

Grocery savings start before you ever step outside your house; it starts when you plan your menus. After figuring out your menus, compile a shopping list from the menus and recipes you will be preparing for the next week. When appropriate, jot down the amount of food you need to buy. Save shopping time by grouping similar grocery items together when you make your list. Then, organize the groups according to their location in the supermarket for easy reference.

Check newspaper advertisements for specials on items you can use; mark the brand name and advertised price on your list. If a store runs out of a special, be sure to ask for a rain check.

Also, whenever possible compare the prices of staple items in several markets, including food warehouses, co-ops, and food thrift stores; stock up on staples when the price is "right."

Collect coupons and group them according to your list. Remain flexible enough, however, to take advantage of any unadvertised specials you may find that will fit into your budget.

Be sure to make your list as complete as possible before you leave home and then follow your list closely. This helps prevent impulse buying and extra trips to the store for items you forgot.

Check the ends of aisles for good buys as well as advertised new products.

Shop quickly. The longer you're in the store, the greater your chance of making unplanned purchases. Save both time and money by avoiding aisles that offer items you don't need. Also, shop after you've eaten; it'll be easier then to resist buying items that look good.

## 7 Savvy Tricks

Here are seven great ways to polish your money-saving skills every time you shop:

1. When buying canned goods, keep their intended use in mind. When shape, uniformity of size, and color of a product are unimportant, use the thriftiest form.

2. Learn to compare prices. Many times a store will take a loss on certain items, like margarine, in hopes you'll do more shopping on other items that are not on sale or are more expensive.

3. Use prepared nonfat dry milk for cooking and baking. Or, mix equal parts of regular fluid milk and prepared nonfat dry milk for drinking. Remember, nonfat dry milk keeps for months in a cool, dry place. Evaporated milk is another economical choice. Substitute evaporated milk for regular milk in cooking by combining equal amounts of evaporated milk and water.

4. Compare domestic and imported cheeses for the best value. Purchase wedges or blocks over sliced, packaged cheeses.

5. Margarine in a tub costs more than stick margarine; both cost less than butter. When nothing but butter will do, buy it in bulk and quarter it.

6. Experiment with store brands and generic foods. In some cases, you may like them as much as the more expensive items.

7. Compare the unit price of foods in different-size containers. Particularly check the foods you use regularly to determine if the "large economy size" is the best buy. Figure the unit price by dividing the price by the number of units (ounces, pounds, or the like) to find the cost per unit. First check the shelves though; the unit price is sometimes posted.

## Old-Fashioned Meat Savings

In days gone by when your grandmother wanted a delicious pot roast for dinner, she visited the neighborhood butcher. She could count on his sound advice and expert ability to provide her with the best cut of meat—at the best buy for the dollar. Although most neighborhood butchers are gone, selecting the best cut of meat—at the best buy for the dollar—can be just as easy in today's supermarkets.

With the variety of prepackaged meats ready for inspection, you can start your selection by quickly glancing at each package of meat. Check the degree of waste (bone, gristle, and fat) on the cuts of meat you're interested in. The best cut is the one with the least bone, gristle, and fat. If you don't see a cut you like, talk to the butcher behind the counter. He may be willing to cut a piece of meat you prefer at no extra charge.

## Pound for pound

Consider the economy of a cut. This is determined by the amount of cooked lean meat (and consequently the number of servings) you get for the price you pay. As a general rule, if you count about three ounces of cooked lean meat as a serving, you will get:

- About four to five servings per pound from meat with little or no fat or bone (ground meat, round steak, lean stew meat, boneless ham, or boned roast).
- Three to four servings per pound from cuts with moderate amounts of bone, gristle, and fat (roasts, chops, steaks, poultry, or bone-in ham).
- Two to three servings per pound from cuts with lots of bone, gristle, and fat (rib chops, spareribs, or chicken wings and backs).

These guidelines help you figure the cost per serving. Divide the cost per pound (as per label) by the number of servings. You may find that a high-priced meat cut with little or no waste is a better buy than a low-priced cut with more bone, gristle, and fat.

# Picking Produce

Sun-kissed fruits and vegetables are the perfect addition to any meal. Choose fresh produce when the supply is greatest; that's also when prices are lowest. It's an economical way to enjoy garden-fresh produce the whole year through.

When shopping for produce, no matter what time of year, select the pick of the crop. It's a waste of both your time and money if you have to cut out bad spots or discard poor-quality produce.

The chart at right identifies the best time of year for particular produce items. The numbers on the chart represent a monthly percentage of the total annual supply of each item. For example, 9 percent of the yearly supply of apples is available in January. If a zero is shown for an item, that fruit or vegetable is not readily available during that particular month.

# Availability of Fresh Produce

**Percentage of Total Annual Supply**

| | Jan. | Feb. | Mar. | Apr. | May | June | July | Aug. | Sept. | Oct. | Nov. | Dec. |
|---|---|---|---|---|---|---|---|---|---|---|---|---|
| **Apples** | 9 | 9 | 10 | 9 | 8 | 6 | 3 | 4 | 9 | 12 | 10 | 11 |
| **Apricots** | 0 | 0 | 0 | 0 | 7 | 58 | 29 | 6 | 0 | 0 | 0 | 0 |
| **Asparagus** | * | 7 | 25 | 34 | 20 | 9 | * | * | 1 | 2 | 1 | 0 |
| **Beans, Snap** | 6 | 5 | 6 | 9 | 10 | 12 | 11 | 10 | 9 | 8 | 7 | 7 |
| **Beets** | 5 | 5 | 8 | 7 | 7 | 11 | 13 | 12 | 10 | 9 | 7 | 6 |
| **Blueberries** | 0 | 0 | 0 | 0 | 2 | 24 | 48 | 24 | 2 | 0 | 0 | 0 |
| **Broccoli** | 9 | 8 | 12 | 8 | 8 | 8 | 7 | 5 | 7 | 8 | 9 | 11 |
| **Brussels Sprouts** | 13 | 12 | 11 | 8 | 4 | * | * | 2 | 6 | 14 | 16 | 13 |
| **Cabbage** | 9 | 8 | 10 | 9 | 9 | 9 | 7 | 7 | 8 | 8 | 8 | 8 |
| **Cantaloupes** | * | * | 3 | 4 | 9 | 19 | 24 | 23 | 12 | 4 | 1 | * |
| **Carrots** | 10 | 9 | 10 | 9 | 8 | 8 | 7 | 7 | 8 | 8 | 8 | 8 |
| **Cauliflower** | 8 | 7 | 9 | 9 | 8 | 7 | 6 | 6 | 8 | 12 | 11 | 9 |
| **Cherries, Sweet** | 0 | 0 | 0 | 0 | 6 | 42 | 46 | 6 | 0 | 0 | 0 | 0 |
| **Corn, Sweet** | 3 | 2 | 4 | 7 | 16 | 18 | 17 | 14 | 7 | 5 | 4 | 3 |
| **Cranberries** | * | 0 | 0 | 0 | 0 | 0 | 0 | 0 | 10 | 25 | 45 | 20 |
| **Cucumbers** | 6 | 5 | 6 | 9 | 11 | 13 | 12 | 9 | 7 | 8 | 8 | 6 |
| **Grapefruit** | 12 | 12 | 13 | 11 | 9 | 6 | 3 | 3 | 4 | 7 | 10 | 10 |
| **Grapes, Table** | 3 | 2 | 4 | 3 | 2 | 6 | 10 | 19 | 19 | 15 | 10 | 7 |
| **Lemons** | 8 | 7 | 8 | 8 | 9 | 10 | 10 | 10 | 8 | 7 | 7 | 8 |
| **Lettuce** | 7 | 8 | 9 | 9 | 9 | 9 | 9 | 9 | 8 | 8 | 8 | 7 |
| **Mushrooms** | 9 | 8 | 9 | 8 | 9 | 8 | 7 | 8 | 8 | 8 | 9 | 9 |
| **Nectarines** | * | 1 | * | 0 | * | 19 | 32 | 30 | 16 | 1 | 0 | 0 |
| **Oranges** | 12 | 11 | 12 | 11 | 10 | 7 | 5 | 4 | 4 | 5 | 8 | 11 |
| **Peaches** | * | * | * | * | 6 | 23 | 29 | 27 | 13 | 1 | 0 | 0 |
| **Pears** | 7 | 6 | 7 | 6 | 5 | 4 | 4 | 13 | 16 | 14 | 10 | 8 |
| **Peas, Green** | 13 | 15 | 11 | 11 | 13 | 14 | 8 | 5 | 3 | 2 | * | 4 |
| **Peppers, Bell** | 8 | 7 | 7 | 8 | 9 | 10 | 10 | 9 | 9 | 8 | 8 | 7 |
| **Pineapples** | 7 | 7 | 11 | 10 | 12 | 13 | 10 | 7 | 4 | 5 | 6 | 8 |
| **Potatoes** | 9 | 8 | 9 | 8 | 8 | 8 | 8 | 8 | 9 | 9 | 8 | 8 |
| **Radishes** | 9 | 8 | 11 | 12 | 11 | 9 | 7 | 6 | 5 | 5 | 9 | 8 |
| **Rhubarb** | 8 | 15 | 17 | 22 | 21 | 10 | 2 | 1 | 1 | 1 | 1 | 1 |
| **Spinach** | 9 | 9 | 11 | 10 | 9 | 9 | 6 | 6 | 7 | 8 | 8 | 8 |
| **Squash** | 7 | 6 | 6 | 8 | 9 | 10 | 9 | 9 | 9 | 9 | 10 | 8 |
| **Strawberries** | 2 | 3 | 8 | 19 | 29 | 16 | 9 | 5 | 4 | 2 | 1 | 2 |
| **Sweet Potatoes** | 9 | 8 | 9 | 8 | 4 | 3 | 2 | 5 | 9 | 11 | 19 | 13 |
| **Tangerines** | 19 | 11 | 9 | 5 | 1 | * | * | 0 | * | 6 | 20 | 28 |
| **Tomatoes** | 7 | 6 | 8 | 9 | 11 | 10 | 11 | 9 | 7 | 8 | 7 | 7 |
| **Turnips and Rutabagas** | 12 | 10 | 10 | 8 | 5 | 4 | 4 | 5 | 8 | 11 | 13 | 10 |
| **Watermelons** | * | * | 1 | 3 | 12 | 28 | 29 | 18 | 6 | 1 | * | * |

*Supply is less than 0.5 percent of annual total
Chart provided courtesy of United Fresh Fruit and Vegetable Association

# Nutrition Analysis Chart

Use these analyses to compare nutritional values of different recipes. This information was calculated using Agriculture Handbook Number 456, published by the United States Department of Agriculture, as the primary source.

In compiling the nutrition analyses, we made the following assumptions:
- For all of the main-dish meat recipes, the nutrition analyses were calculated using weights and measures for cooked meat.

- Garnishes and optional ingredients were not included in the nutrition analyses.
- If a marinade was brushed over a food during cooking, the analysis includes all of the marinade.
- When two ingredient options appear in a recipe, calculations were made using the first one.
- For ingredients of variable weight (such as "2½- to 3-pound broiler-fryer chicken") or for recipes with a serving range ("Makes 4 to 6 servings"), calculations were made using the first figure.

| | Per Serving | | | | | | Percent USRDA Per Serving | | | | | | | | |
| --- | --- | --- | --- | --- | --- | --- | --- | --- | --- | --- | --- | --- | --- | --- |
| | Calories | Protein (g) | Carbohydrate (g) | Fat (g) | Sodium (mg) | Potassium (mg) | Protein | Vitamin A | Vitamin C | Thiamine | Riboflavin | Niacin | Calcium | Iron |
| **Appetizers and Beverages** | | | | | | | | | | | | | | |
| Egg Drop Soup (p. 59) | 25 | 2 | 2 | 1 | 396 | 20 | 3 | 3 | 1 | 1 | 2 | 0 | 1 | 2 |
| Hot Sippin' Cider (p. 77) | 90 | 0 | 23 | 0 | 2 | 180 | 0 | 0 | 2 | 2 | 2 | 1 | 1 | 5 |
| Oriental Soup (p. 59) | 19 | 1 | 4 | 0 | 590 | 176 | 1 | 38 | 10 | 1 | 2 | 1 | 2 | 3 |
| Seafood Dip (p. 109) | 155 | 5 | 4 | 13 | 229 | 93 | 8 | 14 | 2 | 2 | 4 | 3 | 4 | 1 |
| Sweet and Sassy Sipper (p. 41) | 141 | 0 | 36 | 0 | 2 | 207 | 0 | 0 | 17 | 2 | 3 | 1 | 1 | 7 |
| Tomato Sipper (p. 41) | 88 | 2 | 22 | 0 | 365 | 433 | 3 | 29 | 62 | 7 | 4 | 8 | 1 | 9 |
| Wine Spritzers (p. 109) | 113 | 0 | 11 | 0 | 5 | 90 | 0 | 0 | 0 | 0 | 1 | 1 | 1 | 2 |
| **Breads** | | | | | | | | | | | | | | |
| Buttermilk Crepes (p. 100) | 81 | 2 | 5 | 6 | 85 | 43 | 3 | 5 | 0 | 3 | 4 | 2 | 3 | 2 |
| Buttermilk Egg Braid (p. 29) | 106 | 3 | 18 | 2 | 153 | 48 | 5 | 2 | 0 | 10 | 8 | 6 | 2 | 4 |
| Corn Bread Stuffing (p. 74) | 209 | 3 | 22 | 12 | 319 | 114 | 5 | 10 | 3 | 7 | 6 | 4 | 5 | 5 |
| Corn Sticks (p. 35) | 204 | 5 | 28 | 8 | 311 | 99 | 8 | 5 | 0 | 11 | 9 | 5 | 7 | 6 |
| Double Apple-Corn Muffins (p. 35) | 147 | 3 | 22 | 6 | 176 | 76 | 5 | 3 | 1 | 7 | 5 | 3 | 3 | 4 |
| Garden Patch Bread (p. 71) | 83 | 3 | 13 | 3 | 78 | 86 | 4 | 7 | 3 | 7 | 4 | 4 | 2 | 3 |
| **Desserts** | | | | | | | | | | | | | | |
| Almond Tea Cakes (p. 59) | 61 | 1 | 9 | 2 | 56 | 13 | 1 | 2 | 0 | 3 | 2 | 2 | 1 | 1 |
| Bumper Crop Shortcake with Cherry-Banana Filling (p. 71) | 287 | 5 | 43 | 11 | 229 | 290 | 8 | 11 | 16 | 13 | 10 | 8 | 8 | 7 |
| Bumper Crop Shortcake with Strawberry-Rhubarb Filling (p. 71) | 266 | 4 | 37 | 11 | 229 | 207 | 7 | 10 | 54 | 11 | 11 | 8 | 11 | 9 |
| Cherry-Chip Turnovers (p. 11) | 269 | 3 | 37 | 13 | 91 | 40 | 5 | 2 | 1 | 12 | 7 | 7 | 2 | 10 |

| | Per Serving | | | | | Percent USRDA Per Serving | | | | | | | |
|---|---|---|---|---|---|---|---|---|---|---|---|---|---|
| | Calories | Protein (g) | Carbohydrate (g) | Fat (g) | Sodium (mg) | Potassium (mg) | Protein | Vitamin A | Vitamin C | Thiamine | Riboflavin | Niacin | Calcium | Iron |

**Desserts** (continued)

| | Calories | Protein (g) | Carbohydrate (g) | Fat (g) | Sodium (mg) | Potassium (mg) | Protein | Vitamin A | Vitamin C | Thiamine | Riboflavin | Niacin | Calcium | Iron |
|---|---|---|---|---|---|---|---|---|---|---|---|---|---|---|
| Chocolate Cheesecakes (p. 95) | 200 | 4 | 18 | 13 | 141 | 79 | 6 | 12 | 0 | 1 | 7 | 1 | 3 | 3 |
| Chocolate-Filled Meringues (p. 95) | 459 | 8 | 74 | 17 | 145 | 255 | 12 | 13 | 2 | 4 | 15 | 1 | 13 | 7 |
| Chocolate-Macaroon Cupcakes (p. 53) | 132 | 2 | 19 | 6 | 90 | 53 | 3 | 1 | 0 | 0 | 2 | 0 | 2 | 2 |
| Luscious Lemon Torte (p. 109) | 407 | 5 | 59 | 17 | 146 | 60 | 7 | 7 | 5 | 2 | 5 | 1 | 3 | 4 |
| Individual Alaskas (p. 115) | 198 | 4 | 33 | 6 | 98 | 101 | 6 | 3 | 1 | 2 | 8 | 1 | 6 | 2 |
| Oat Wafers (p. 11) | 32 | 1 | 5 | 1 | 12 | 20 | 1 | 1 | 2 | 2 | 1 | 1 | 0 | 1 |
| Orange Soufflés (p. 83) | 159 | 5 | 14 | 9 | 111 | 110 | 7 | 12 | 18 | 6 | 8 | 2 | 4 | 5 |
| Orange Spice Bars (p. 89) | 109 | 1 | 18 | 4 | 65 | 91 | 2 | 3 | 9 | 4 | 2 | 2 | 1 | 3 |
| Peach Ice (p. 47) | 118 | 1 | 30 | 0 | 3 | 221 | 2 | 13 | 24 | 2 | 2 | 5 | 1 | 2 |
| Tutti-Frutti Cobbler (p. 17) | 162 | 2 | 33 | 3 | 249 | 184 | 3 | 3 | 20 | 7 | 4 | 6 | 1 | 5 |
| Upside-Down Sugar-and-Spice Cake (p. 17) | 356 | 3 | 46 | 19 | 243 | 133 | 5 | 9 | 2 | 4 | 3 | 1 | 6 | 4 |

**Main Dishes**

| | Calories | Protein (g) | Carbohydrate (g) | Fat (g) | Sodium (mg) | Potassium (mg) | Protein | Vitamin A | Vitamin C | Thiamine | Riboflavin | Niacin | Calcium | Iron |
|---|---|---|---|---|---|---|---|---|---|---|---|---|---|---|
| Beef and Bean Soup (p. 32) | 417 | 19 | 32 | 24 | 765 | 724 | 29 | 16 | 32 | 17 | 12 | 21 | 6 | 23 |
| Chicken and Cheese Pockets (p. 8) | 283 | 18 | 20 | 14 | 197 | 255 | 27 | 14 | 11 | 9 | 13 | 17 | 15 | 8 |
| Chicken and Dumpling Stew (p. 97) | 401 | 24 | 42 | 15 | 1002 | 644 | 38 | 33 | 46 | 26 | 26 | 35 | 26 | 17 |
| Country Strata (p. 38) | 434 | 30 | 22 | 25 | 668 | 458 | 46 | 29 | 45 | 14 | 36 | 22 | 37 | 16 |
| Eggs and Sausage Scramble (p. 103) | 244 | 13 | 7 | 18 | 342 | 282 | 19 | 18 | 22 | 17 | 18 | 6 | 6 | 13 |
| Ham-Sprout Kabobs (p. 89) | 423 | 23 | 29 | 22 | 652 | 990 | 35 | 8 | 135 | 39 | 17 | 28 | 4 | 20 |
| Hearty Ham and Potato Chowder (p. 86) | 397 | 24 | 22 | 23 | 986 | 787 | 37 | 94 | 41 | 35 | 25 | 21 | 19 | 18 |
| Herbed Chicken and Vegetables (p. 97) | 391 | 29 | 39 | 11 | 190 | 306 | 45 | 132 | 17 | 32 | 37 | 48 | 6 | 26 |
| Lemony Fish Dinner (p. 56) | 197 | 26 | 11 | 5 | 369 | 565 | 40 | 35 | 81 | 9 | 12 | 16 | 7 | 8 |
| Meat and Spinach Range-Top Casserole (p. 20) | 632 | 31 | 21 | 48 | 697 | 710 | 48 | 128 | 39 | 69 | 35 | 29 | 38 | 28 |
| Mini Loaves with Beer-Cheese Sauce (p. 26) | 282 | 18 | 15 | 16 | 439 | 264 | 27 | 12 | 11 | 6 | 14 | 18 | 8 | 13 |
| Nutty Rice-Stuffed Chicken (p. 106) | 343 | 36 | 22 | 13 | 214 | 420 | 55 | 138 | 31 | 15 | 29 | 58 | 22 | 22 |
| One-Dish Stroganoff (p. 23) | 471 | 26 | 27 | 28 | 244 | 407 | 40 | 13 | 7 | 25 | 26 | 35 | 8 | 21 |
| Orange-Sauced Chicken (p. 92) | 211 | 29 | 16 | 3 | 62 | 204 | 44 | 6 | 73 | 10 | 15 | 55 | 4 | 11 |
| Pick-a-Pot Pie (with Ham, Corn, and Parmesan Points) (p. 117) | 359 | 16 | 23 | 23 | 703 | 317 | 25 | 12 | 20 | 25 | 16 | 18 | 10 | 12 |
| Pizza Spuds (p. 65) | 329 | 12 | 41 | 14 | 717 | 921 | 18 | 3 | 80 | 15 | 11 | 19 | 8 | 13 |
| Pork and Vegetable Dinner (p. 80) | 297 | 15 | 12 | 20 | 715 | 421 | 23 | 81 | 51 | 23 | 12 | 15 | 4 | 15 |
| Reuben-Style Strata (p. 41) | 485 | 30 | 24 | 30 | 1242 | 468 | 46 | 22 | 8 | 25 | 37 | 14 | 41 | 19 |
| Roast Turkey (p. 74) | 334 | 50 | 0 | 13 | 0 | 0 | 77 | 40 | 0 | 12 | 60 | 75 | 3 | 29 |
| South-of-the-Border Bundles (p. 50) | 395 | 19 | 46 | 16 | 475 | 494 | 29 | 23 | 38 | 24 | 19 | 11 | 32 | 23 |

| | **Per Serving** | | | | | | **Percent USRDA Per Serving** | | | | | | | |
| --- | --- | --- | --- | --- | --- | --- | --- | --- | --- | --- | --- | --- | --- | --- |
| | Calories | Protein (g) | Carbohydrate (g) | Fat (g) | Sodium (mg) | Potassium (mg) | Protein | Vitamin A | Vitamin C | Thiamine | Riboflavin | Niacin | Calcium | Iron |
| **Main Dishes** *(continued)* | | | | | | | | | | | | | | |
| Speedy Tuna Salad (p. 14) | 272 | 21 | 9 | 17 | 757 | 539 | 32 | 24 | 31 | 9 | 16 | 34 | 18 | 12 |
| Spicy Peach-Glazed Ham (p. 89) | 286 | 18 | 11 | 19 | 638 | 212 | 27 | 0 | 1 | 27 | 9 | 15 | 1 | 13 |
| Stuffed Steak Rolls (p. 112) | 259 | 24 | 3 | 16 | 137 | 330 | 37 | 17 | 30 | 6 | 13 | 23 | 4 | 17 |
| Summer Stir-Fry (p. 68) | 231 | 22 | 13 | 10 | 298 | 457 | 33 | 79 | 110 | 12 | 30 | 34 | 7 | 16 |
| Sweet and Sour Beef (p. 44) | 295 | 25 | 9 | 17 | 375 | 361 | 39 | 8 | 20 | 5 | 13 | 21 | 3 | 20 |
| Zesty Pork Pizza (p. 62) | 564 | 23 | 46 | 32 | 1257 | 291 | 35 | 5 | 29 | 56 | 23 | 26 | 20 | 22 |
| Zucchini-Cheese Frittata (p. 53) | 282 | 18 | 8 | 20 | 351 | 293 | 28 | 33 | 13 | 8 | 27 | 2 | 27 | 13 |
| **Salads** | | | | | | | | | | | | | | |
| Cool Cucumber Salad (p. 109) | 114 | 1 | 18 | 5 | 23 | 227 | 2 | 9 | 23 | 3 | 3 | 2 | 3 | 6 |
| Cranberry Apple Mold (p. 77) | 200 | 0 | 51 | 0 | 2 | 59 | 0 | 1 | 8 | 1 | 1 | 0 | 1 | 2 |
| Curried Macaroni Salad (p. 65) | 210 | 3 | 20 | 13 | 277 | 138 | 5 | 45 | 7 | 11 | 6 | 6 | 4 | 4 |
| Fruit Fix-Up (p. 65) | 81 | 0 | 21 | 0 | 5 | 180 | 1 | 3 | 10 | 2 | 1 | 2 | 1 | 3 |
| Fruit Toss (p. 41) | 207 | 1 | 30 | 11 | 5 | 225 | 1 | 4 | 39 | 5 | 3 | 2 | 3 | 3 |
| Garden Marinade (p. 23) | 85 | 1 | 6 | 7 | 38 | 212 | 2 | 11 | 62 | 3 | 3 | 2 | 2 | 4 |
| Pear Waldorf Salad (p. 77) | 150 | 2 | 20 | 8 | 111 | 237 | 3 | 3 | 11 | 5 | 4 | 2 | 2 | 3 |
| Potato Plate (p. 47) | 95 | 2 | 14 | 4 | 81 | 352 | 3 | 7 | 24 | 5 | 3 | 6 | 2 | 5 |
| Spinach-Iceberg Salad (p. 115) | 129 | 4 | 6 | 11 | 136 | 276 | 6 | 53 | 34 | 5 | 9 | 2 | 7 | 9 |
| Tropical Fruit Fandango (p. 103) | 71 | 1 | 17 | 1 | 1 | 180 | 1 | 3 | 45 | 6 | 2 | 2 | 3 | 3 |
| Very Berry Salad (p. 83) | 86 | 3 | 18 | 1 | 34 | 187 | 4 | 1 | 46 | 2 | 8 | 2 | 10 | 3 |
| **Miscellaneous** | | | | | | | | | | | | | | |
| Cranberry Syrup (p. 103) | 47 | 0 | 8 | 2 | 25 | 18 | 0 | 2 | 4 | 0 | 0 | 0 | 1 | 1 |
| Honey Spread (p. 35) | 108 | 0 | 7 | 9 | 112 | 7 | 0 | 8 | 0 | 0 | 0 | 0 | 0 | 0 |
| Peanut-Honey Spread (p. 35) | 60 | 2 | 4 | 5 | 56 | 45 | 3 | 2 | 0 | 2 | 1 | 4 | 0 | 1 |
| Peanut Pilaf (p. 115) | 244 | 6 | 29 | 12 | 241 | 126 | 9 | 8 | 5 | 11 | 2 | 16 | 2 | 7 |
| Peanutty Topper (p. 53) | 39 | 1 | 4 | 2 | 17 | 37 | 2 | 0 | 0 | 1 | 0 | 3 | 0 | 1 |
| Pineapple-Cheese Topping (p. 103) | 28 | 1 | 1 | 2 | 16 | 12 | 1 | 2 | 1 | 0 | 1 | 0 | 1 | 0 |
| Savory Rice Mix (p. 26) | 121 | 2 | 27 | 0 | 136 | 52 | 4 | 3 | 7 | 2 | 1 | 3 | 1 | 2 |
| Strawberry Sauce (p. 23) | 50 | 0 | 12 | 0 | 4 | 15 | 0 | 0 | 1 | 0 | 0 | 0 | 0 | 1 |